SANKOFA

SANKOFA

Celebrations for the African American Church

Grenaé D. Dudley

Carlyle Fielding Stewart III

United Church Press

Cleveland, Ohio

United Church Press, Cleveland, Ohio 44115
© 1997 by Grenaé D. Dudley and Carlyle Fielding Stewart III

Printed in the United States of America on acid-free paper

02 01 00 99 98 97   5 4 3 2 1

Library of Congress Cataloging-in-Publication Data
Dudley, Grenaé Denise McDuffie, 1952–
     Sankofa : celebrations for the African American church / Grenaé
  D. Dudley, Carlyle Fielding Stewart III.
       p. cm.
     Includes bibliographical references and discography.
     ISBN 0-8298-1179-6 (pbk. : alk. paper)
     1. Afro-Americans—Religion. 2. Afro-Americans—Rites and
ceremonies. I. Stewart, Carlyle Fielding, 1951– . II. Title.
BR563.N4D83 1997
264'.089'96073—dc21   97-5600
                                                           CIP

To: *Rosebud McDuffie, who is truly one of the mothers of the church.*

Brandon and Rachel Dudley, who always wanted to know how many pages.

Frederick Donaldson, Claudia McDuffie, and Claude McDuffie, who listened, loved, and supported this project.

Darriell McKeithen, who has always been a spiritual advisor and supporter.

Those individuals who allowed us to use our ceremonies as they celebrated special life events: Nicki Moss; Bernadine Williams; Phares and Karen Noel; Ken, Jackie, and William Lewis; the members of Hope United Methodist Church, and the Sunday school class of What's Happenin' Now!

Thanks Joi!

Reverend Wendell Anthony, keeper of the flame

John Kwame Porter

The memory of the Rev. Willie Robinson Smith, my brother in Christ, who fought the good fight and finished the race, and the memory of Ulysses Duke Jenkins, who loved his people and kept the faith.

Dr. Grenaé Dudley, one of the great minds of this country, whose heart and soul went into this project.

CONTENTS

Introduction

One of the most progressive forces in African American communities is the African American church. A fulcrum of spiritual vitality and empowerment, and a vehicle for social and political protest, the African American church has been a beacon of light to black people in America. From the era of slavery to the present day, the black church and African American spirituality have critically shaped the consciousness, values, ethos, and culture of African American people and enabled them to survive with dignity in their struggle for integrity, personhood, liberation, and wholeness.

Moreover, a significant aspect of the black church's influence in the cultural and spiritual formation of African Americans is the manner in which ritual has energized black life, ordered the chaos of black existence, and provided African Americans with a firm foundation for spiritual, psychological, and cultural growth in the wake of cultural dislocation.

Molefi Asante reminds us that the struggle of African Americans has been to relocate ourselves culturally in a land which has dislocated us from our African cultural roots and traditions.[1] Asante, one of the forerunners of the Afrocentric movement, affirms the value of culture as a tool for a people's self-actualization.

Thus, the African American church has always been a vital cultural center in African American communities. It is here that the symbols and ritual dramas of black life are actualized, cultivated, and ceremonialized. It is within the veil of the black church that African Americans have created, interpreted, articulated, and preserved the cultural and spiritual traditions of both African American people and their African ancestors.

The recent rise of the Afrocentric movement, inspired in part by Ron Karenga, Molefi Asante, and others, has ignited a fervent coalescence of the cultural remnants of Africa with those of African American traditions. We are indebted to such scholars and practitioners for urging us to unapologetically reclaim those ritual practices which are essential to the long-term survival and sanity of African Americans as a people in America.

Accordingly, we believe that the black church must continue to be a cultural and spiritual center, calling us back to the central claims of our faith. This occurs through inculcation of the values, beliefs, and practices which encourage cultural and spiritual creativity and further empowers people to realize their greater human potential, both as individuals and as a community.

This book delineates some African-based celebrations for the African American church. Its purpose is to help black congregations relocate themselves within the framework of African spiritual consciousness and culture and to provide a blueprint for various African-based ritual ceremonies. These rituals not only historically and culturally reconnect us with important remnants of our African past, but also ground us within the cultural traditions fostered by African American spiritual praxis.[2]

Many of these ceremonies were designed for specific occasions at Hope United Methodist Church, Southfield, Michigan. Some originated from special requests of the members, while others were added because we felt they could contribute to our knowledge about who we are as a people. We hoped to boldly demonstrate that our history and culture should be joyfully celebrated, not shrouded in shame and secrecy. Creating the ceremonies around traditions and beliefs was critical because it added meaning and memory-making emotion.

The twin tiers of our cultural-spiritual formation are: 1) the ability to reclaim the vital traditions of our African ancestors through rituals which symbolize and signify the deeper meanings of our cultural, spiritual, and social formation as a people, and 2) the cultivation, preservation, and incorporation of those rituals into the practice and structure of African American church ceremonies for the perpetuation, advancement, and consolidation of community.

The black church has preserved, sustained, and combined the dynamics and forms of African spiritual, cultural, and ritual traditions into its own ritual ceremonies and practices. Thus, it has done more to preserve, translate, and synthesize African ritual and ceremony into a bona fide African

American spiritual and cultural presence than any other institution in America.

The ceremonies in this book are not limited to specific denominations, but are designed to be used by anyone interested in practicing and celebrating African-based ceremonies. While this effort does not exhaust the full spectrum of African-based celebrations in African American churches, it will provide the celebrants with ideas which can inspire a greater cultural appreciation and sensitivity to African-based traditions.

AFRICAN AND AFRICAN AMERICAN RITUALS AND CEREMONIES

Rituals and ceremonies serve to help us remember our history and the importance of recognizing the sacrifice and work of previous generations. African Americans have a unique history in that we are a product of our African heritage as well as our African American roots. To go beyond the roots of slavery and reach for our magnificent heritage as Africans allows us to experience the grandeur and splendor of the diverse African people and our true cultural background.

As the quintessential cultural archive of African American communities, the African American church is that sacred place where the ancient rituals and ritual dramas of African life have been unabashedly conceived, practiced, and preserved. Within the matrices of the black church and African spirituality, purpose, value, and communal solidarity win out over sorrow, alienation, and social disintegration.

The rituals and ceremonies that follow focus on the treasures of our past, the gifts of our present, and the attainment of what is to come.

The Significance of
African-based Rituals in the
African American Church

*To ritualize life, we need to learn how to invoke the spirits
or things spiritual into our ceremonies.*

—MALIDOMA PATRICE SOMÉ,
Ritual, Power, Healing, and Community

R itual has always been a significant part of the African
and African American experience. It celebrates our connection with divine reality by harmonizing the community and creating an ethos of symbiosis, which is the
foundation of human interaction. Dona Richards, in an article
on African American spirituality, explains:

> The ultimate expression of the African world view is the
> phenomenon of ritual. Only through ritual can death
> be understood as rebirth. It is through ritual that new

life was given to the African spirit. We performed and experienced ritual drama in North America.[1]

The black church creates the context for ritualizing the dramas of black life and culture, and creates a place for their perpetual celebration. In black worship, music, preaching, singing, praying, teaching, testifying, celebrating, shouting, dancing, healing, and communing, we find the essence of ritual in the African American experience. Ritual is also actualized in rites of passage programs and the various traditions of the black church, such as men's and women's days, Kwanzaa, and other observances which reflect a holistic concern for African American church life and culture.

Remnants of African traditional religion and culture are often found in the worship ceremonies and other ritual dramas of the black church. These traditions include call and response patterns as well as holy shouts, dances, and other expressive forms of worship. Ritual also has historical importance because it not only allows blacks to connect with and preserve African cultural traditions in a strange land, but it also gives them the means to order the chaos and uncertainties of their American experience. The development and practice of ritual connects black people with the larger cosmos and invokes the presence of divine reality as a framework for the formation and continuation of black consciousness, behavior, and belief. Ritual consolidates and elevates consciousness through practice in community and calls attention to the community's corporate strength through its collective awareness. Thus ritual provides an ultimate reference point for the consolidation and unification of African peoples.

Victor Turner has done significant work on the importance of ritual in human community and employs the term *luminality* to define those interim phases of rites of passage between which individuals move toward various stages of life.[2] In this respect ritual helps secure a spiritual and cultural stability for persons in the larger community amid the terrors and complexities of their existential condition. Within the parentheses of our sojourn as a people in America, we have discovered a place of solidarity and continuity which has helped us establish our place in the larger universe. Ritual has thus enabled African Americans to develop some cultural, spiritual, and ontological stasis in a world of turmoil, upheaval, and flux created by racism, oppression, and other forms of devaluation and dehumanization.

The African American church is that continual place where those rituals that give black people purpose, vitality, and meaning have largely flourished. The function of ritual then is to provide for what Monroe Fordham terms "adaptive and expressive needs."[3] Ritual has enabled blacks to adapt to their peculiar milieu and express and address needs within those communities which reflect their ultimate concerns. The adaptive function of ritual also allows black people to use ritual as an instrument of self-actualization and empowerment.

From the days of slavery's hush harbor (worship meetings held by slaves in secret) and campfire meetings to the present-day rituals of the African American church, blacks have communed in order to interpret and articulate their humanity and faith through the cultivation and practice of ritual dramas. These ritual dramas create a close relationship between meaning and interaction, fueling the dynamics of human empowerment. Participants are thus inspired to continue to face and overcome the daily challenges and absurdities of their human condition.

Dona Richards describes the significance of those early ritual encounters:

> We gathered and enjoyed the warmth of our commonness, of our togetherness. We would form a circle each touching those next to us so as to physically express our spiritual closeness. We "testified.". . . As we laid down our burdens . . . we began to understand ourselves as communal beings, no longer the kind of persons that the slave system tried to make of us. Through our participation in these rituals, we became one. We became, again, a community.[4]

The actualization of ritual through the practice of African American spirituality consolidated the early slave communities and provided what Emile Durkheim termed *solidarity* among the people, thwarting the devastations of dehumanization fomented by white racism and oppression.[5] Without ritual, African Americans could not have developed those systems of literal and figurative meaning which symbolize their quest for community, the actualization of potential, and the realization of full personhood in America.

Ritual has other significant functions in African American communities as well. It encourages critical reflection on the past and the development of processes of enculturation and deculturation which ensure long-term survival. Consistent ritual practices engender the formation of values and community, the establishment of cultural, behavioral, and ethical norms which reinforce the power, purpose, and destiny of human beings. Ritual also helps to normalize the boundaries of context indispensable to the emergence, formation, and continuation of community. The dynamics of ritual, therefore, are essentially empowerment processes which confer value, meaning, and vitality. Moreover, they provide black people with a sense of the sacred within the continuum of human history.

Perhaps of all the important things rituals signify, processes of empowerment are most prominent because they enable individuals to establish the cultural, spiritual, relational, and communal links essential to their long-term survival. For centuries, the rituals of black religion, spirituality, and the black church have enabled African Americans to overcome the odds and cruelties they faced, and thus have been a saving grace.

The following African-based rituals have emerged from years of research and consultation with numerous individuals both within and outside of the African Diaspora. It is our hope that they will become part of the ongoing empowerment of African Americans as we celebrate our cultural and spiritual traditions as a people within the frameworks of our respective denominations and faiths.

The Common Elements
of African and African American
Ceremonies and Celebrations

Human life has another rhythm of nature which nothing can destroy. On the level of the individual, this rhythm includes birth, puberty, initiation, marriage, procreation, old age, death, entry into the community of the departed and finally entry into the company of the spirits. On the community or national level, there is the cycle of the seasons with their different activities like sowing, cultivating, harvesting and hunting. The key events or moments are given more attention than others, and may often be marked by religious rites and ceremonies.

—JOHN S. MBITI, *African Religions and Philosophies*

T his is exactly our purpose—to mark events in our lives as African Americans with spiritual ceremonies that allow us to remain anchored to our past as we press on toward the future. In designing these ceremonies and celebrations, the key has been to understand various African concepts and philosophies and filter them through our living experiences as blacks in America. The ceremonies are designed to evoke deep emotions and to symbolize commitment. Our desire is to have them become part of our tradition and our legacy to our children. They are meant to remind us of our history and heritage and to give us a vision of what we will become.

Sankofa

There are recurring concepts that appear throughout the ceremonies and celebrations. One is the concept of *Sankofa,* which means, "in order to know where you are going you have to know where you have been." It is symbolized by a bird whose feet face forward and whose head looks back over its shoulder. The purpose of *Sankofa* is to remind us to keep an eye on the past as we continue to move ever forward.[1]

Habari Gani?

The second concept is the question *Habari gani?* which means "What is the news?" Dr. Maulana Karenga, founder of Kwanzaa, includes this question in his celebration on each day of Kwanzaa. It is a greeting one extends to another. The response to the greeting is the particular part of the *Nguzo Saba,* the name for the seven principles of Kwanzaa, that corresponds to that day. (*See Kwanzaa Celebration and Kwanzaa Service, pp. 77–88.*) It is important for us here because it elicits an interaction beyond just a hello. It opens communication with mutual understanding and serves as a call and response. The call is always *Habari gani?;* the response will be different for each different ritual.

Calling the Village

A third recurring concept is calling the village. The villagers are the *community* of witnesses and extended family who serve an integral role in the ceremony or celebration. The role of the village is to accept the transition and agree to support it and to serve as witnesses that the event has occurred. Calling the village represents the shared responsibility we all have for one another.

Pouring Libations

The fourth concept is pouring libations. Our interpretation of this ceremony is that it is a way in which we pay homage and link a particular ritual to the concept of *Sankofa*. It is a way to honor and remember those in our past, to acknowledge our present, and to salute our future. After each area has been addressed, water (or milk) is poured either into the earth directly or into a container. After the ceremony, the content is then poured into the ground. According to Mbiti the acts of pouring libation to the past are symbols of communion, fellowship, and remembrance.[2]

Others

Other common elements in the rituals are invoking the spirit, dramatizing the spirit's presence and powers as a life-giving and sustaining force through music, song, and dances.

These African concepts will appear in the rituals that follow, but, as mentioned earlier, they will be filtered through our experience as African Americans so we can claim them as our own.

RITUALS FOR THE STAGES OF LIFE

Rituals that mark transitions in life are ceremonies that are related to events that are universal and occur (and may recur) over the course of a lifetime. They include Naming of Child Ceremony, Baptism Ceremony, Youth Confirmation Ceremony, Rites of Passage, The Wedding Ceremony, Renewal of Wedding Vows Ceremony, Ritual for House Blessing (*Nyumba*), A Celebration of Elders Ceremony, and Funeral Ceremony: A Celebration of Life.

In ancient societies, various processes of socialization culminated in the celebration or observance of various life stages and cycles. Today these celebrations are less prominent, but they remain an important part of the African community's vitality and identity. Celebrating these transitions helps us to not only remember them but also to enhance their meaning in our lives so that we do not undertake them lightly. Each ceremony forces us to commit to the transition and sends a message to the entire "village" that this transition has taken place and everyone is to pay appropriate homage and respect.

Naming of Child Ceremony

Background

The birth of a child is an exciting and sometimes overwhelming event that brings high expectations. It is important to remember God's hand in such a miraculous event. The birth of a child is one of the greatest gifts of all and is honored with a naming and dedication ceremony that is held as soon as possible. The ceremony can be held in the church, the hospital chapel, in the hospital room, or, in the case of a home birth, at the mother's bedside. The name of the child is given by its father and mother and is held in confidence until the time of the ceremony. Because the ceremony acknowledges genealogy—the past, the present, and the future—it is important for the baby's grandparents or other elders to be present. Each grandfather determines an important trait he would like to pass on to the child. For example, a grandfather may feel he has a strong work ethic which he would like to pass on; or he may wish to pass on a gift of wisdom or a strong faith in God. Any quality that will be helpful to the child in life may be passed on. The minister's closing words and gesture appear in a ceremony described in *Roots* by Alex Haley.

Participants

- child
- parents
- grandparents or other available elders
- minister(s)
- family or community

Materials

- altar
- libations apparatus
- oil
- recorded music (optional)

In Advance

- The parents agree on a name for a child.
- Each grandfather decides on a trait to pass on to the child.
- The libation apparatus is placed on the altar.
- A song may be chosen by the family to sing together or to play from a recording at the ceremony's closing (optional).

The Ceremony

After the parents inform the minister that all participants are present, the minister enters and stands at the altar.

Minister: I call the family together to name the newborn child of (*parents' names*). I call the parents and grandparents to take their places for the "passing."

Parents and grandparents gather around the altar.

MINISTER (*holding the child*): The strength, power, and links of genealogy.

Minister pours libations in respect for the past and past generations while offering a prayer of thanksgiving for the past.

MINISTER (*passing child to paternal grandfather*): What do you pass on to this child?
PATERNAL GRANDFATHER: I pass on (*name of trait*).

Paternal grandfather passes the child to maternal grandfather.

MINISTER: What do you pass on to this child?
MATERNAL GRANDFATHER: I pass on (*name of trait*).

Maternal grandfather passes the child to the father.

MINISTER: The child is passed to the present.

Minister pours libations to the present and to the future and offers a prayer of thanksgiving for the present and the future.

MINISTER (to the father): What have you to pass to this child?
FATHER: A name.
MINISTER: What is the significance of this name? What will you call this child?
FATHER: The first name passed to this child means _____ and is (*the family's last name*). The child's chosen name means _____ and will be (*the child's first name*). The child's middle name represents _____ and will be (*the child's middle name*).

Father passes the child to the minister, who anoints the child with oil and offers a prayer of dedication.

MINISTER (*holding the child toward heaven and speaking directly to the child*): Behold, my (*son/daughter*), the only thing greater than thyself!

Passes the child to the mother with blessings for the parents to nurture and raise the child in God's ways.

The ceremony may be concluded with the family singing or by playing recorded music (optional).

Baptism Ceremony

Background

Baptism is an important ritual in the Christian church. It celebrates not only the gift of procreation, but also God's sanction of the continuation of human life. Water is commonly used in rituals throughout Africa and remains an important element in African traditional society. Water, the basis of all life, is ritually poured out to symbolize cleansing and purification, "not only of bodily but mystical impurities contracted through broken taboos, the commitment of crime, and contamination by evil magic or curse."[1]

Water, according to the Dogon, is equally the supreme life force of nature. "God molded the earth with water. Blood too is made out of water. Even in stone there is this force, for there is moisture in everything."[2] The Dogon are a people of the Sudan whose cosmogony, metaphysics, and religion have been equated with the peoples of antiquity. Although considered by some to be primitive, a thorough study of their culture has revealed some of the cultural progress, subtleties, and sophistication of modern civilization.

The value of water as a purifying life force is reinforced in the Old and New Covenants. Water and Word are significant symbols in the Genesis creation stories as well as the creation stories of the religions of Africa. The common elements of these various viewpoints reside in the significance of water as a life-purifying force for restoration, cleansing, and redemption. Such assumptions undergird both the Christian view of baptism and the African idea of water as purification.

The baptism ceremony may be celebrated in the church or outside at a stream, lake, river, or some other watering place which has historical or religious significance in the life of the community. Baptism is a communal event in which all members of the community joyously participate.

Participants

+ child
+ parents
+ minister(s)
+ elder or storyteller
+ members of the community

Materials

+ *kikombe* (libation) cup or bowl on small table
+ traditional African attire
+ recorded music or live instrumentalists (optional)
+ dancers (optional)

In Advance

+ Encourage those who will participate in the processional to wear traditional African attire to the ceremony.
+ Invite individuals to participate in the Litany of Prayers for the Child.

The Ceremony

The baptism ceremony has several distinct parts, all of which lead to the baptism ritual itself.

The Gathering

Before entering the sanctuary or baptismal area, the elders, minister, and family members gather to invoke the presence of God through prayer. A representative from each significant group in the community may be called upon to raise a prayer on behalf of the child to be baptized and the child's family. The prayers should stress the importance of the community's support of the child and family in their sojourn of faith. Prayers invoking awareness of ancestral presence may be also be offered. The veneration of ancestors is an important dimension in naming, baptizing, and rites of passage for various members of the community.

The Processional

Minister(s), elders, family members, and significant others, dressed in African attire, process by threes into the sanctuary or baptismal area, symbolizing past, present, and future. Traditional church hymns or other music may be played during the processional or trumpeters, drummers, and other instrumentalists may play African, African American, Caribbean, or Latin sacred music. The processional may also be accompanied by dancers, acolytes, or others who can both lead and fol-

low the line of celebrants. The entire community stands for
the processional. After everyone has processed into the baptismal area, the entire congregation is seated.

The Litany of Prayers for the Child

A minister offers a prayer of consecration or a prayer of communal invocation. A community elder offers a prayer of hope
and preservation for the child and family. A family member
offers a prayer invoking the memory and support of ancestors and ancestral spirits. Finally, a child representing the
younger generation offers a prayer of strength and guidance
for the future.

Gifting the Child and Libations

At this time a variety of spiritual gifts may be offered as praise
and celebration for the life of the child. Music, dance, or
some other offering may signify the promise and hope of this
child as a member of the faith community.

After these spiritual offerings, several children or adults
may come forth to the small table at the center of the room
and pour libations from the *kikombe (umoja)* cup to express
a prayer or wish for a particular gift or quality of character
they hope the child will display as he or she grows into man-
hood or womanhood.

Telling the Family Story

An elder, family member, or community storyteller may come
forth and share significant highlights of the history of the
child's family, its legacy and heritage, and important or outstanding ancestors and their achievements. The story highlights the sojourn of the child's forebears and raises expectations about the child's present and future. At this time the

parents may wish to share information about the meaning and significance of the child's name, any revelations or miracles which may have occurred during the course of the birth or as a result of it, and any other important expectations or information which will illuminate the importance of this child as a created person of God. This is a time of reflection—an homage to the past and the anticipation of the child's future.

Prayers of Preparation

The minister may follow with various prayers of preparation, petition, and supplication for the child.

The Baptismal Ritual

MINISTER: People of great joy, strength, and promise, we have come together as one community of faith to celebrate God's continuation of creation in the presence of this child, (*child's name*). God has given us this most esteemed of all gifts. Therefore, we as a community must do all in our power to unearth, nurture, cultivate, sustain, and multiply the resources and potential of the created of God. We recognize the gift of baptism as a rite of purification, symbolizing our entrance into spiritual union with Jesus Christ our God, Savior, and Liberator, who was baptized by John in the Jordan, and who embodied in his person all the great promises, gifts, and potential of the new creation. It is therefore with great joy that this family and community present (*child's name*) for the rite of baptism in anticipation that this child will grow to be all that God called (*him/her*) to be in the fullness of time.

Let us pray: Great God of the Universe, Ancient of Days, the most high and beneficent God, God of all glory and promise, we gather in this place to life our praise for your power and design to take this child and use (*him/her*) for your glory, promise, and purpose. We ask today, God, that you make (*him/her*) into a faithful disciple.

PEOPLE: Hear our prayer, God of creation!

MINISTER: We pray, God, that you give (*child's name*) a mind to cultivate to use (*his/her*) potential, the strength to persevere in the spirit of (*his/her*) ancestors, the faith to keep ultimate trust in you, the resiliency to withstand the tides of adversity, the compassion to feel and be in solidarity with others, the integrity to honor and respect (*his/her*) elders, and the courage to admit (*his/her*) errors and frailties. We pray, God, that your hand will lead, guide, energize, and temper (*him/her*) on this journey of life.

PEOPLE: Hear our prayer, God of life!

MINISTER: We ask, God, that your will prevail in all things in (*his/her*) life, that your Spirit infuse (*him/her*) with clear-headedness and right-heartedness, that the wisdom and strength of (*his/her*) wisest ancestors fall upon (*him/her*) like fresh dew on morning glories, that justice, truth, love, and mercy envelop, surround, and oversee (*his/her*) steps all along (*his/her*) path.

PEOPLE: Hear our prayer, God of wisdom, knowledge, and justice!

MINISTER: We pray, Creator God, that (*child's name*) will have the faithfulness of Abraham, the boldness of Moses, the empathy of Queen Esther, the temerity of Mordecai, the vision of Joshua, the tenacity of Nehemiah, the gift of Jeremiah, the vision of Isaiah, the tenderness of Ruth, the courage of King David, the gratitude of Paul, the aptitude of Solomon, the fortitude of Deborah, the commitment of

Aquila and Priscilla, the bravery of Stephen, the inheritance of Timothy, and the power, grace, and love of Jesus.

PEOPLE: Hear our prayer, God of love, truth, and power!

MINISTER: As you have brought our spiritual and familial ancestors through the trials by storm and fire, bring your child to safekeeping in your hands!

PEOPLE: Hear our prayer, God of history and deliverance!

MINISTER: We ask that your blessings be upon this child and (*his/her*) family, community, and nation. May (*he/she*) take (*his/her*) rightful place among the people of God and make a difference throughout the land.

ALL: Hear our prayer, God of hope and peace!

MINISTER: Let the families come forth with (*child's name*).

Family members and sponsors come forward and place the baby in the arms of the minister.

MINISTER (*raising the child with both hands above his head*): We raise this child unto you, God, as a sign of your favor, promise, love, joy, and goodness. We raise this child as a symbol of hope. We raise this child as a symbol of our gratitude to you. We raise this child as a symbol of all you hope and expect from us and all yet unrealized in us that will be fulfilled in (*child's name*). Amen.

MINISTER (*lowering the child*): (*Child's name*), I now baptize you in the name of the Father, the Son, and the Holy Spirit. May God's power work forever within you and may you be a faithful disciple of Jesus Christ!

MINISTER (extending child toward community): Members of the household of God and this community, I give you (*child's name*) as a child of your own to be nurtured, encouraged, loved, and protected as your own. Do every-thing in your power to train and sustain (*him/her*) in the love and faith of Jesus Christ, now and forever. Amen.

The minister places the child in a family member's arms.
Songs of praise, jubilation, and celebration may be offered.

A final prayer, lead by a family member, minister, or another community member, may be offered before the recessional.

Youth Confirmation Ceremony

Background

Many churches require their youth to attend confirmation classes to study the Word and learn the disciplines of their faith. After students have successfully completed the confirmation course, a ceremony may be conducted during the worship service. The students should receive copies of the ceremony in advance so they can preview what will take place, understand what they will say, and memorize the necessary passages. They should be strongly encouraged to think about why they deserve to be confirmed and accepted as full members of the church.

Participants
- youth being confirmed
- their parents or guardians
- confirmation leader and teacher(s)
- minister

Materials

- copies of the ceremony
- African attire
- libation apparatus
- recorded music (optional)
- confirmation certificates and gifts

In Advance

- Distribute copies of the ceremony to the participants.
- Help youth prepare traditional African attire to wear during the ceremony.

The Ceremony

Like the Baptism Ceremony, the Youth Confirmation Ceremony has several distinct parts.

Vows of Acceptance

As the ceremony begins, the youth and their teachers are seated with their families in the congregation.

MINISTER: A group of (*number*) youth have spent the last (*number*) weeks studying, questioning, and learning the principles of their faith. They know that through the sacrament of baptism they are initiated into Christ's holy church. Through water and the Spirit they are born again and are saved through Jesus Christ.

This village of (*name of church*) will open the doors to these youth and bring them into full membership in the faith. So before this village we must present them, approve them, question them, accept them, and confirm them. Through confirmation, we renew the covenant declared at our baptism, acknowledge what God is doing for us, and affirm our commitment to Christ's holy church.

Presentation of the Candidates

The youth are brought before the congregation.

MINISTER: Will the teachers who have taught these youth please come forward. (*Contines as teachers come forward.*) It is through their commitment to our youth and dedication to the future of this village that this confirmation is possible.

MINISTER (*after teachers have assembled at the front of the church*): Who presents the youth for confirmation?

CONFIRMATION LEADER: On behalf of the teachers and parents (*and guardians*), I present these youth for confirmation. They were told to "study to show themselves approved." They have done so.

The leader may continue with personal memories that demonstrate the candidates' commitment to confirmation.

MINISTER: Will all the candidates for confirmation please rise? When your name is called, please take your place before this village of (*name of church*).

As each name is called, the candidate walks down the middle aisle to take a place in a semicircle on the altar. After the last candidate is in place, the minister takes a position in front of the group and addresses them.

MINISTER: On behalf of this entire village, this congregation of *name of church,* I ask you: Do you accept the freedom and power God gives you to resist evil, injustice, and oppression in whatever forms they present themselves?

YOUTH: I do.

MINISTER (*addressing the congregation*): Will you nurture these youth in Christ's holy church, that by your teaching and example they may be guided to accept God's grace for themselves, to profess their faith openly, and to lead a Christian life?

CONGREGATION: I will.

MINISTER (*turning back to the youth*): Will you from this day forward, through the blessings bestowed upon you, represent this village and your faith? At every opportunity walk the walk and know not only who you are but *whose* you are?

YOUTH: I will.

MINISTER: Do you believe in God?

YOUTH: I believe in God Almighty, maker of heaven and earth.

MINISTER: Do you believe in Jesus Christ?

YOUTH: I believe in Jesus Christ, God's only child, who was conceived through the Holy Spirit, was born of the virgin Mary, suffered under Pontius Pilate, was crucified, died, and was buried. He descended to the dead. On the third day, he rose again; he ascended into heaven, is seated at the right hand of God, and will come again to judge the living and the dead.

MINISTER: Do you believe in the Holy Spirit?

YOUTH: I believe in the Holy Spirit, the holy Christian church, the communion of saints, the forgiveness of sins, the resurrection of the body, and life everlasting. Amen.

Pouring of Libations
The pouring of libations connects the new church members with the church's past and future.

MINISTER: I take this *umoja,* the cup of unity, and I pass it on to the one of you who is the most worthy. Who has studied and has shown himself or herself to be approved?

The minister passes the cup to the first youth, who accepts the cup.

FIRST YOUTH: (*Minister's name*), I accept this unity cup because I am worthy, because (*adding a vow as a personal witness to Christian faith and experience*). But I pass it on to (*name of the next person in line*) because (*he/she*) is also worthy.

The next candidate accepts the cup.

NEXT YOUTH IN LINE: I accept this unity cup because I too am worthy, because (*add vow*). But I pass it on to (*name of the next person in line*) because (*he/she*) is also worthy.

Continue until every youth has spoken.

LAST YOUTH IN LINE: I accept this cup because I too am worthy because (*add vow*). I, however, pass this unity cup back to you, (*minister's name*), for we are all worthy.

MINISTER: I accept this *umoja* cup for this confirmation class of (*month and year*), and I find you all to be worthy. On behalf of this village and before the hosts of heaven, I pour libations on your behalf. I toast the past (*adding personal memories from the church's past, including the contributions of parents and grandparents, a historical figure of the church, or other meaningful information*).

We recognize you today in the spirit of our biblical and familial ancestors who have all made their rites of passage in the faith. By study, prayer, and diligent inquiry, you have now come to this place to be confirmed in the Christian

church. You have made safe passage, and you have demon-
strated the courage, humility, determination, resiliency, intelligence, faith, perseverance, tenacity, capacity, and verac-
ity which seemingly will make your journey complete.

But there are many more roads to tread, many more av-
enues yet unexplored, many more challenges which await
you along faith's way. Can you complete this journey as
your ancestors before you completed their tasks so that we
might have this present moment? They came through fires,
storms, trials, troubles, captivity, slavery, Jim Crow, segrega-
tion, persecution, discrimination, prosecution, alienation,
castration, frustration, dehumanization, denigration, dese-
cration, humiliation, violation in every possible form, and
virtual obliteration, but it was because of their faith and belief in almighty God, their absolute unwavering, undaunted
belief in a God of love, liberation, and salvation that they
were able to withstand the storms of life.

Like Abraham, they were dared to step out in faith and
did. Like Moses, they would not let the thought of personal
imperfections deter them from their course of action. Like
Esther, they had compassion for their people. Like Daniel,
Shadrach, Meschach, and Abednego, they withstood the
fiery furnace of racism and persecution. Like Joshua, they
kept a good report against great odds. Like Nehemiah, they
had a mind for building and rebuilding that which had fallen
down because of neglect. Like Stephen, they stood against
the stones of threat and the threat of stones. Like Aquila and
Priscilla, they kept their commitment to God in the face of
great odds. Like David, they stood on the promises of God
despite their own sin and indiscretions.

You have come from that people. You have come from the Garveys, Mandelas, Bethunes, and DuBois; from the Hamers, Wellses, Douglasses, and Washingtons; from Jackie Robinsons and Wilma Rudolphs; from the Latimers, McCoys, and Bannekers; from the Martin Kings, from the Ruler of rulers, from the Medgar Everses and Malcolm Xs, from men and women of vision, power, and promise. You have come from that people!

So we pour the libation in tribute and honor to those great souls and forces who have come this far along the way, embracing the God of our weary years, the God of our silent tears. I pour libations to the present (*adding personal observations about the church's present*).

I pour libations to the future. To each and every candidate who has been found to be worthy. You are the future of this village. Commit to it with your time, your talent, and your tithes (*adding personal observations about the commitments that will help the church in the future*).

Will the parents (*and guardians*) of these youth please stand. These are your children, and they represent the love, care, guidance, and faith you have bestowed upon them. Thank you for bringing your children to Christ. But the job is not over. Do you vow to continue to teach these children the Word of God?

PARENTS: I do.

MINISTER: Do you accept their faith and acceptance of the Holy Spirit in their lives?

PARENTS: I do.

MINISTER: Are you committed to their continued growth, and will you see to it that they commit their time and talents for greater good?

PARENTS: I will.

Reception

The youth are welcomed into their new roles as full and active members of the church.

MINISTER (*addressing the congregation*): You may be seated. To the village of (*name of church*), I present to you the new members of the village. They have been initiated into the faith and have committed themselves to become servants of God. Your charge is to teach them well. Let the example you set be the one you expect them to follow.

By the power vested in me, I bestow upon them all the rights and privileges of membership. Please rise and welcome our newest members into this village.

The congregation stands and applauds and the music begins. As the youth return to their seats, they shake the minister's hand and are given a certificate of membership and a gift from the church. The confirmation leader and teachers assist in this process. The new church members return to their seats.

Rites of Passage

*Knowledge is like a garden. . . . If it is not cultivated,
it cannot be harvested.*

—GUINEAN PROVERB

Background

Many cultures recognize stages children pass through on their way to being accepted as adults. Starting at a very young age, children are prepared for their adult role in life and are taught the necessary skills. The process is time-consuming and is supported by all the adults in the community. Once all rites of passage are completed, the youth becomes a young adult with all the responsibilities and privileges this role demands. According to Kelvin Seifert and Robert Hoffnung:

> In societies that still have relatively simple, agricultural economies and traditional cultural and social arrange-

ments, this transition is fairly smooth and predictable, and grows out of a long period of preparation. For example, when a teenaged Australian Aborigine goes on his year-long walkabout through the desert, with only a few simple weapons to protect him, his chances of returning safely are high, because much of his childhood has been spent in learning skills that help to meet this challenge.[1]

In modern industrial societies such as ours, however, the process is far more complicated. Seifert and Hoffnung go on to say that our rites of passage tend to be more symbolic than real, and the transition from childhood to adulthood can be difficult and prolonged. Helping our youth become and remain focused is part of a process that should involve the whole church community. Principles, values, and morals are key concepts in a rites of passage program. When a ceremony is part of the process, the point of transition is clearly marked.

Some modern churches have a rites of passage program that may last several sessions to one year. To implement the rites of passage ceremony that is described here, the process must involve parents and guardians and/or mentors, proceeding always with the recognition that no child grows to adulthood without the support, discipline, encouragement, and mentoring of an adult who serves as a guide. It is this adult parent, guardian, or mentor who will present the child for passage.

In designing the ceremony, a great deal of thought went into visualizing the passage. The result—the concept of creating a "passage" with the adult sponsors—clearly represents a true transition.

The ceremony should be presented before the church—the entire village. Members without children should be encouraged to attend. Young children should also attend and witness the ceremony. It is important that the entire village be informed. At the initial ceremony conducted at Hope United Methodist Church in Southfield, Michigan, our local newspaper covered the event, printing names and pictures from the ceremony. This recognition gave importance to the event and helped confirm it as a true rites of passage celebration.

Sankofa

The rites of passage ceremony is an African American celebration that makes use of both our past and present by involving dancers to perform African dances or having stilt walkers available to lead the processional and create a festive atmosphere. The ceremony also involves percussionists—drummers who clear the way and set the tone. Appropriate Afrocentric attire for all the dancers and performers is essential. The entrance of the performers through all available entrances creates a lively, joyful atmosphere. A storyteller may tell a story relevant to the occasion.

Participants

- minister
- director of the Rites of Passage Program
- teachers and assistants
- mentors
- children
- dancers or stilt walkers
- drummers
- storyteller (optional)

Materials

- printed programs, which include the names of the Kwanzaa principles and their meanings
- gong
- music (*See suggested selections below.*)

In Advance

- Help children prepare African traditional attire.
- Decorate chairs and arrange them at the front of the hall.
- Have youth prepare and rehearse their roles.

Song Suggestions

- Lift Every Voice and Sing
- Can You See a Brand New Day? (from *The Wiz*)
- Celebration (Kool and The Gang)

The Ceremony

The Village Is Called

Prior to the start of the ceremony, the church bell rings once a minute for fifteen minutes. Inside the hall a gong is sounded three times to signal everyone to be seated and silent. The church bells are used to alert the community that something special is about to happen. It symbolizes calling the village together for an important meeting. Everyone is alerted for miles around. Ringing the bells prior to the ceremony lets everyone know to hurry because the ceremony is about to begin. The gong indicates that the doors are closing and the ceremony is imminent.

Calling the Elders

Once the tone has been set, music is played as the following people enter: the minister, director of the Rites of Passage

Program, teachers and assistants, and mentors. All these individuals take their places at the front of the hall, where chairs, draped dramatically and festively, have been arranged.

Calling the Rites of Passage Participants

Once all the elders have taken their places, the doors in the back of the hall open and all members of the village stand. Solemnly and quietly, the rites of passage participants enter, dressed in African attire and walking to a steady drum beat. They proceed to the front and stand in front of their chairs, facing their mentors.

Proclamation

After all participants are in place, the minister asks everyone to be seated and states that the village is gathered to witness this ceremony and welcome into adulthood these children who have proven themselves worthy. The minister then explains the meaning of manhood/womanhood, its obligations and responsibilities to elders, men, women, children, race, community, and nation.

MINISTER (*to the youth*): Who is requesting passage and why?
YOUTH (*rising one at a time and speaking individually, in turn*): I am (*name*). I am requesting passage because I am worthy.

The youth, in turn, go on to explain why they feel they are worthy. Their statements should be well thought out and well rehearsed. They should be convincing and truly reflect the youth's worthiness to make the passage.

MINISTER (turning to the director, teachers, and mentors): Who presents these children for passage? (*All teachers and mentors stand.*)

DIRECTOR: As leaders of the Rites of Passage program, we have witnessed the growth of these children, the formulation of their goals, their respect for their elders, others, and themselves, their hunger for knowledge, their spiritual development, and their commitment and demonstration of the concepts of the *Nguzo Saba,* the seven principles of Kwanzaa: *Umoja, Kujichagulia, Ujima, Ujamaa, Kuumba, Nia,* and *Imani.*

PASTOR: Then I say to each of the mentors and teachers that I accept your recognition that each of these children is ready to walk the passage. But the key to opening the passage is the contribution—in talent, time, and gifts—we can expect from each of these children present.

The Call and Response

MINISTER: Who presents this child, (*name of child*), for passage, and why does (*he/she*) deserve to cross?

The child stands in front of the minister, who places his or her hands on the child's shoulder. The mentor shares observations about the child and tells why the child deserves to cross. The words should be meaningful and specific to the child. The mentor will need to think a great deal about these words that will help this child make the transition. When each mentor finishes, the child stands in front of the mentor. After the final child has been addressed, the mentors speak collectively to the minister.

MENTORS (*together*): We present these children for passage with God's blessing and before the witnesses of this village.

The minister addresses the children, speaking to them briefly about what crossing the passage means, accepting their state-

*ments about why they feel they should be permitted to cross,
and acknowledging the mentors' statements. The minister
gives the children the opportunity to refuse passage, saying, "If
you feel you are not ready, say so now!" Then the minister asks
the mentors to take a step back and the children to turn, face
the mentors, and take two steps back.*

MINISTER: Mentors, observe the distance between you and
the children. The distance is symbolic—it is wide enough
that you are unable to hold on to the child and must now
let go! Children, observe the distance between you and
your mentors. It is narrow enough for you to seek advice,
assurance, and guidance without being forced or controlled.
It allows you to comfortably make your own decisions.
Now, please turn and face the village.

I present before this village these children, their teachers, and their mentors. They have told you they are ready.
If there are any reasons why anyone in this village feels
these children are not worthy, speak now!

*At this point, planned or spontaneous questions may be raised.
All questions should be directed to the children and they
should answer for themselves.*

The Passage

MINISTER: I find these children to be worthy. Mentors,
please form the passage.

*The mentors space themselves on both sides of the aisle, forming
a passage. The village rises and faces the center aisle. Children
slowly walk down the aisle to music, looking each mentor in
the eye and acknowledging the mentor with a nod of the head.*

Meanwhile, festive music, dance, or songs (such as "Can You See a Brand New Day?" from The Wiz*) acknowledge the transition. The young adults then walk up the side aisle to the altar and stand in front of the previously vacated mentors' seats. When they have all returned, the minister presents the new young adults to the village.*

Conclude with a reception to honor the young adults.

The Wedding Ceremony

A home without a woman is like a barn without cattle.
Woman without man is like a field without seed.

—ETHIOPIAN PROVERB
FROM CHARLOTTE AND WOLF LESLAU, *African Proverbs*

Background

Wedding ceremonies are a way of telling the world that two people have made a commitment to one another to start their lives together. It is an announcement that their status has changed and that they are entitled to all the privilege and recognition that goes with that change. The wedding ceremony should be dramatic, emotional, and meaningful to the couple. Both partners should be involved in the planning as their first major task together. The following ceremony has several nontraditional aspects that make it memorable and dramatic.

Preferably the setting for this ceremony is a church, but the ceremony can be held in a garden setting as well. The music should be provocative, with contemporary as well as traditional styling. This is an African American celebration, so the decorations should reflect Africa. The bridal party should be encouraged to wear African attire.

Participants

+ bride and groom
+ parents
+ ushers
+ minister
+ dancers

Materials

+ table
+ libations apparatus
+ white batons with white streamers
+ music

In Advance

+ Set up a special table that includes a cup and receptacle for the pouring of libations. The table should be strategically placed so it can be seen but will not interfere with the wedding party.
+ Choose traditional African attire for the wedding party.

The Ceremony

The Parents' Processional

During the song "Somewhere Out There" the mothers are escorted to their seats by ushers outfitted in African attire.

Invocation and Words of Welcome

The minister comes to the altar alone, addresses the congregation, extends the welcome, and instructs the congregation about what is expected of them as participants in the ceremony.

MINISTER: The welcome that is extended here is for all who are present and for those loved ones who have gone before but still live in the hearts and minds of (*bride and groom*) who are to be joined here today.

The minister says a prayer based on Genesis 2:23–24.

MINISTER: Therefore a man leaves his father and his mother and clings to his wife and they become one flesh. You come here today to serve as witnesses to a rite of passage that marks a significant change in the lives of (*bride and groom*). They are about to commit to one another their lives, their hopes, and their vision. As she becomes joined with him, it is she who will know her husband and he, his wife. This time has been chosen for me to give you your charge as witnesses. You must decide if you will obligate yourself to this charge as family and friends. Given that you will, your charge is that you must look upon this union with hope and excitement. You must share now in their joy and remind them of this day when times become difficult for them. You must encourage them to cling to one another and know that the tie that binds is God's love for them and their love for one another. You must tell all who do not know that no one is to come between them, and you must respect the holiness of their union, for in Christ the two will become one. Will you serve as witnesses to this wedding and faithfully carry out your charge? If you feel you cannot carry out this charge, speak now or forever hold your peace. If you can commit, please answer by saying I will.

CONGREGATION: I will.

Pouring Libations to the Past

MINISTER: Libations will be poured throughout this ceremony as a toast to the past, the present, and the future. Pouring libations is a way to honor those who have gone before and who have made this ceremony possible; to toast to the present, the family members and friends who are gathered here today; and to toast to the future, pouring libations to the couple and their future together.

I now pour libations to the past, to the relatives and friends who love us and who are no longer with us in body but are with us in love and spirit. (*The minister continues by including names of loved ones important to the couple.*) To those who have gone before, I pour libations to you.

The minister pours libations into a chalice set up on the altar.

The Dance

Dancers dressed in white and carrying white batons with white streamers appear in the sanctuary, moving to music such as "Caravena" (instrumental from *Mystere Cirque Du Soleil*) or "Joyful, Joyful" (*Sister Act II*) that is upbeat and short. They dance a dance that is symbolic of sweeping, praise, and inviting the spirit to bless this place. A dance school can be contacted or a professional dance troupe. A troupe that includes children would be best. The dancers' outfits should be flowing, their movements fluid and consistent with where they are and appropriate for the occasion.

When the dance is completed, the dancers disappear as quickly as they arrived.

The Groom's Processional

This processional is unique in that the groom and the groomsmen process down the aisle. They process to the music of "Egypte" (instrumental from *Mystere Cirque Du Soleil*). The procession is regal and establishes the groom as the head of the family to be. He pays homage to the gathering of family and friends by walking down the aisle and slightly nodding to both sides very regally, walking with control, intent, and dignity. The groomsmen process in pairs at some distance behind the groom. In sanctuaries that have no center aisle, the groom comes down one aisle while the groomsmen are positioned across the other aisles and process in together, giving the groom a distinct lead. The minister is waiting near the center of the altar, and the groom kneels for his blessing as the groomsmen take their places in formation facing the altar.

Prayer for the Groom

As the music continues softly in the background, the minister says a brief prayer for the groom, emphasizing his intent and calling upon God to give him the strength he will need to establish himself as head of the household he is about to establish.

MINISTER: The choice you are about to make is a serious one, and you have given this much thought because you have chosen as your mate the woman who will love you, who will comfort you and serve as your strength. She will be your confidante and friend. She will stand beside you to face what comes, she will stand behind you to push you on, and she will stand in front of you to pull you forward. She is bone of your bone and flesh of your flesh. Love her, cherish her, and protect her always.

The groom stands and takes his place next to the groomsmen during the song "When I Fall in Love."

The Bride's Processional

There is a brief moment of silence as all prepare for the coming of the bride. The doors open in the back of the church, but no guests are seated during this time. To the music of "Caravena" (from *Mystere Cirque Du Soleil*), the bridesmaids process down the aisle. The groomsmen meet them about two-thirds of the way down the aisle, each bowing slightly to one of the bridesmaids and extending his arm. Each groomsman escorts a bridesmaid to her place and then takes his own place. When all attendants are in their places, the ushers roll out the white runner. The music shifts, and the song for the bride, "Kalimando" (instrumental from *Mystere Cirque Du Soleil*), begins playing.

The flower girl processes down the aisle, dropping white rose petals on the runner. When the bride is about to enter, the minister signals for all to rise. The bride and her father or escort walk slightly over halfway down the aisle, and the groom walks down the aisle to meet them. As they meet, all pause.

GROOM: I ask your permission, sir, to continue this journey with (*bride's name*). I know you have been with her and brought her this far, but I can take her and protect her for the rest of this journey.

The father turns and faces his daughter, who acknowledges the groom's words with a nod. The father steps aside, motions for the groom to take his place, and places the arm of the bride on the arm of the groom. The father steps behind the couple, follows them to the altar, and stands there as they take their place in front of the minister. The couple kneels, and the minister says a prayer. Then the minister gives the sermonette.

MINISTER: I will leave you with words of our ancestors that serve to guide and teach. They are proverbs to impart wisdom and understanding of the commitment you are about to make: Love is like a baby; it needs to be treated tenderly and if you offend, ask for pardon; if offended, forgive. I ask you now to stand and take the vows of marriage. Who gives this woman to be married to this man?

FATHER (OR ESCORT): I do.

Father (or escort) takes his seat.

The Charge

MINISTER: I require and charge you both, as you stand in the presence of God, before whom the secrets of all hearts are disclosed, that having duly considered the holy covenant you are about to make, you do now declare before this company your pledge of faith, each to the other. Be assured that if these solemn vows are kept inviolate, as God's Word demands, and if steadfastly you endeavor to do God's will, God will bless your marriage, will grant you fulfillment in it, and will establish your home in peace.[1]

Minister, speaking to each party individually, says the declaration of intent/consent specific to each's faith.

MINISTER: (*Name*), will you have this (*woman/man*) to be your wedded (*wife/husband*), to live together in the holy estate of matrimony? Will you love (*her/him,*), comfort (*her/him*), honor and keep (*her/him*) so long as you both shall live?[2]
BRIDE/GROOM: I will.

Exchange of Vows
The bride and groom may wish to exchange their own vows instead of repeating the vows below.
MINISTER: In the name of God, I take you, (*name*), to be my (*husband/wife*) from this day forward, to have and to hold, for better, for worse, for richer, for poorer, in sickness and in health, to love, honor, and respect; to join with you and to share all that is to come; to give and to receive; to speak and to listen; to inspire and to respond; and in all our life together to be loyal to you with my whole being till death do us part, according to God's holy ordinance; and thereto I pledge my faith.[3]

The bride and groom stand on either side of the minister, who addresses the congregation.

Pouring of Libations to the Present and Future
MINISTER: In that these two have pledged and exchanged vows, it is now that you must make that commitment to love them as one, to hold them to the vows that they have made, and to let no one come between—not family, not friends, not those things real or imagined. Do you as family and friends make this commitment to (*names*)? If so, answer by saying, "I will."
CONGREGATION: I will.

MINISTER: Then I pour libations to you who have made a commitment to uphold the holiness of this marriage and have agreed to support them as one and love them as God has instructed you to do. So, what God has joined together, let no one put asunder.

I now pour libations to (*names*) as they complete this rite of passage. In the name of God, bless this union and let this couple know that you are the tie that binds and that, with you in their lives, they need but ask and it shall be given, seek and they will find, knock and the door will be opened unto them. I pour libations to the future of this couple in God's holy name.

Minister pours the libations.

Blessing and Exchanging of Rings

The minister returns to the couple and stands in front of them.
MINISTER: May I have the rings?

The minister takes the rings and holds them up.

MINISTER: These rings are the outward and visible sign of an inward and spiritual grace, signifying to us the union between Jesus Christ and the church. Bless, O God, the giving of these rings, that they who wear them may live in your peace and continue in thy favor all the days of their lives; through Jesus Christ, amen. (*Return the rings to the couple. Speak to the bride and groom respectively.*) Repeat after me. (*Name*), I give you this ring as a sign of my vow, and with all that I am and all that I have, I honor you. In token and pledge of our constant faith and abiding love, with this ring I thee wed in the name of the Father, and of the Son, and of the Holy Spirit.[4]

Lighting of the Unity Candle

MINISTER: Now light this candle as a symbol of your unity and let this flame serve as the indistinguishable light in your life—a light that points the way to heaven and God's promise to you that no matter how long the night, the morning will soon come.

Song: The Lord's Prayer

Declaration of Marriage

MINISTER (*to the bride and groom*): You have declared your consent and vows before God and these witnesses. It is a covenant that God will bless and fill with goodness and grace. (*To the congregation*) You have served as witnesses to what has taken place here. Go and tell everyone what you have heard and seen because it is now that I pronounce that (*names*) are husband and wife; in the name of the Father, and of the Son, and of the Holy Spirit. Those whom God has joined together, let no one put asunder. (*To the groom*) You may salute your bride.

Communion (Optional)

Benediction

The minister gives the benediction, adding this announcement: May I be the first to introduce to all who are gathered here Mr. and Mrs. (*name*).

Recessional

The recessional repeats the music from the groom's processional, symbolizing that the bride has now joined with the groom.

Renewal of Wedding Vows Ceremony

Background

Marriage is the covenant one makes with another to commit to a collective vision. Renewal of vows after ten years of marriage in today's environment represents a milestone of commitment and dedication to the original vows—"In sickness and in health, until death do us part." A ceremony in honor of such a milestone should be encouraged, not only to rekindle the love, passion, and spiritual growth between the couple, but also to mark the next decade of their journey together. The ceremony also represents to the village and to young people planning to marry that a ten-year journey together is desirable and achievable. This ceremony was designed around the concepts of calling the village, *Sankofa,* and the pouring of libations.

Participants

- couple
- other family members
- minister

Materials

- music that has special meaning for the couple
- if children are present, small gifts
- African attire for the participants

In Advance

- Prepare a video or slide show of memorable moments in the life of the couple.
- Husband and wife prepare words about their marriage to say to each other.
- The elders and couple should not share what they will say to one another before the ceremony, but should meet several times to talk about their feelings and why this renewal is important.

The Ceremony

The Village Is Called

No one enters the sanctuary until the village is called. The call is represented by three peals of a gong or bells of the organ. The three gongs sound to indicate that the village has been called and that the ceremony is imminent. Ringing the gong three times symbolizes that we are about to pay homage to the past the present and the future. Three times also assures that everyone within hearing distance has heard and that they know to move to their places as quickly as possible. There should be a brief pause between each gong to give everyone the message and give time to get in place.

Sankofa

To connect the renewal ceremony with the past, the ceremony begins with the showing of a video or slides of important moments in the couple's life. If possible, the pictures should be set to music. As the last scene is frozen on the screen, a gong is rung three times. The choir marches in, singing a song such as "Siahama (We Are Marching in the Light of God)." After the choir reaches its destination, the village stands.

Calling the Elders

As the music continues, the elders of both families march down the aisle, with the eldest in each family in the lead. They stand in front of their seats near the altar, facing the congregation (village). The elders are followed by the minister.

The Family Enters

The music continues as the children march down the aisle, followed by the parents.

Habari Gani?

MINISTER: *Habari gani?* What is the word? The word is a celebration of the renewal of vows between this couple.

The Call and Response

MINISTER: Who stands as a witness to the declaration of love between (*names*)?
CHILDREN: We do.
ELDERS: We do.

The elders are seated. The children and parents face the minister.

The Proclamation

The minister speaks on the marital relationship, faith, love, and commitment.

The Call and Response

MINISTER (*to the wife*): What have you to say to this man?

Wife turns to face her husband and responds with words she has prepared in advance expressing her love and what their life together has meant to her. She also expresses what her commitment will continue to be.

MINISTER (*to the husband*): What have you to say to this woman?

Husband responds with words he has prepared in advance expressing his love and what their life together has meant to him. He also expresses what his commitment will continue to be.

MINISTER (*to the elders*): What have you to say to this couple?

The man's father responds to the wife. The woman's father responds to the husband. The oldest elder responds to both.

The Pouring of Libations

The minister explains the pouring of libations—a form of paying homage to the past, present, and future. After each salute he or she instructs the village to say *N'sah,* which means to drink.

MINISTER: To the past. To the elders who are present here today, to those in our collective past, and to those in this family's past who are now dead. And to the ones we can no longer remember.

Minister pours water into a container.

VILLAGE: *N'sah.*

MINISTER: To the present. To (*couple's names*) and others of their generation.

Minister pours water into a container.

VILLAGE: *N'sah.*

MINISTER: To the future. To the children who are present here today and to those yet to be born.

Minister pours water into a container.

VILLAGE: *N'sah.*

The Legacy

If children are present, the minister speaks about the importance of family and the legacy passed on through the generations, ending with the following.

MINISTER: For it is through our offspring that we have personal immortality. Our children carry on our name. They will remember us to their children, and their children will remember us to their children. For a person is not dead until forgotten.

Call and Response

This part of the ceremony acknowledges the children and their importance to the village and to our memory.

MINISTER (*to the couple*): What is your legacy to your children?

FATHER: To my son(s), I give (*presenting son(s) with a gift, a small token that has special meaning*).

MOTHER: To my daughter(s), I give (*presenting daughter(s) with a gift, a small token that has special meaning*).

The family embraces. Then the minister calls the elders to embrace the family and addresses the villagers, speaking about their roles in supporting the family and witnessing what has taken place.

MINISTER: To this village I present this family. Do you stand as witness to the renewal of their vows and their recommitment to one another?

VILLAGE: We do.

The family turns to the village and the peace is passed to all present. (Everyone hugs and embraces one another and the family).

PASTOR: May God bless this marriage, this family, and this village.

Ritual for House Blessing
(*Nyumba*)

Background

The home in African traditional communities is a vital and important place of healing, comfort, and restoration. The old adage "a home is a person's castle" probably had its origins in African thought, where it signifies a place of honor and well-being for inhabitants. This ritual may be used to bless a new home or to sacralize a home where residents are invoking a greater awareness of the presence and power of the Spirit of God. If the Holy Spirit resides in the home, it is believed that it can be a place of true harmony and peace.

Hospitality is another important idea in African traditional thought. There are really no strangers in the community, and each home is a place where hospitality (*ukarimu*) is fervently practiced. This ritual underscores the importance of the Spirit's presence and establishes the home as a place of invitation and hospitality.

The family may gather in a significant or central location of the house (the *mahali patakatifu au pa salama*). This is the core (*kiini*) or heart (*moyo*) of the house where the ritual can be celebrated. Some homes in early African American and African communities had sanctuaries or prayer stations. Here the Spirit of God or the ancestral spirits took up predominant residence. Although the Spirit of God permeates the entire structure of the residence, there was one *sanctum sanctorum*—one central and esteemed place where people believe they come into the Spirit's presence. Accordingly, each home should have a sanctuary or designated place where the family gathers for prayer, Bible study, reflection, and meditation. The ritual may occur in this honored room or place, or prayers and blessings may be offered in each room of the house.

Participants

- family members
- minister

Materials

- gifts

In Advance

- Hosts prepare food and other festivities for the reception following the ceremony.
- Guests select house gifts and plan the words they will say during the offering.

The Ceremony

HOSTS: Pastor, we welcome you to our home and invite you to pray that this house will become a home; a place of peace, love, joy and harmony. We pray, Pastor, that God will be the center of this household; that whatever differences arise within these walls, they may be resolved amicably with love and empathy. We pray also, Pastor, that this home will be a place of refuge and renewal for all who live here and all who come here. May it be a place of invitation and hospitality, where each soul can find perfect peace and perfect rest from the noise and furor of the outer world. We thank you and welcome your presence here today.

MINISTER: In the tradition of our African ancestors who emphasized the importance of the home and village, we raise our humble prayers on behalf of this family and this abode. God, we pray that this home will be a place of refuge and peace; a place of love, joy, hope, and faith. May it be a place where the people can freely be and express themselves openly and honestly, without fear of recriminations or reprisals. May it be a place of celebration for life together as a family and life with you as the center of their lives. May it be a place of healing and comfort, of restoration and renewal for the souls of those weary inhabitants and strangers who pass through its doors. May it be a place of prayer and adoration to you. May it be a place where your name and presence are affirmed and lived each day in quiet reflection, in devotion, study and meditation. May it be a place where the spirits of our ancestors may take refuge and comfort in their world. May it be a place where our children can grow and be happy, where our lives together may be sealed and sanctified by your love and for your glory! We raise our prayers in this house today. May every beam and plank be filled with your Spirit. May the brick and mortar exude your presence. May your light shine around and throughout this place, making it a home where Christ could find perfect comfort and peace. Amen.

At this time the people may move to other rooms of the house, offering prayers and blessings in each location. Upon returning to the center, a collective prayer for prosperity and peace may be offered by all. The Lord's Prayer, the Twenty-third Psalm, or another prayer may also be rendered.

Presentation of Gifts

At this time the participants may bestow gifts for the house upon the family. Each person may state the significance of the gift and the purpose for which it is offered, followed by a blessing, hope, or aspiration for the family.

HOSTS (*upon receiving each gift:* We receive this gift as a token of your blessing and love. May we be worthy of this blessing as we make our home a place of love and peace.

After conferring gifts, a final prayer may be offered by the minister to the family and participants. This is followed by celebration with music, food, and other festivities.

A Celebration of Elders Ceremony

Background

The late Dr. Ulysses Duke Jenkins, associate dean of African American Student Affairs at Northwestern University, instituted an event called "An Evening with Our Elders." Various jazz musicians from the Chicago area were invited to celebrate their musical gifts in tribute to outstanding elders in the community who had made a significant contribution to the life of the community.

African society has always held the elders of the community in high esteem. They are the heralds of wisdom and tradition, and they represent various creative life forces within the community. The African American community, particularly in the South, has always stressed the importance of respecting and venerating the elders of the community.

In this day of cultural flux and degeneration, many of the cultural practices which once consolidated the community have increasingly declined. As the extended family and systems of kinship undergo radical transformation, many communities have lost the important tradition of celebrating its elders. We believe the church should play a central role in restoring this time-honored tradition to its ritual and ceremonial practices. While this may be done at any time of year, Black History Month is an appropriate time in which to hold such an observance.

Annually each church should celebrate certain significant elders, both within and outside of the church community, who have made positive contributions to the community. This celebration may be a musical tribute, a banquet with a keynote speaker, or a ritual ceremony incorporated into Sunday worship. The following ceremony is tailored for incorporation into worship or may be used as a separate program for celebration.

Participants

- elders
- narrator
- youth
- drummers, musicians, and/or dancers

Materials

- libations apparatus

In Advance

- Elders and community members prepare symbolic gifts or tokens.

The Ceremony

The Gathering (*Mkutano*)

The narrator may begin with a statement about the significance of elders in African and African American communities. The role of elders in the family and extended family may be underscored, with emphasis on their roles in adjudicating disputes, providing counsel to the young and old, and serving as spiritual guides or mentors to various persons within the community.

NARRATOR: Beloved, we have come together to celebrate the lives of the elders in our community. These individuals have made boundless sacrifices in nurturing, teaching, encouraging, and challenging us all to be better persons and citizens of our communities and nation. Today we gather to pay tribute to these great men and women. Moreover, it is because of their wisdom, spirituality, and sensitivity to the unique gifts and concerns of African American people that we gather here in humble tribute to their legacies.

Telling the Story (*Matangazo*)

NARRATOR: Today we honor the following persons: (*name the individuals and make a brief statement about each elder's field of contribution*).

After the names are called, a brief biography of each elder may be read. The contributions and achievements of each person may be highlighted or dramatized. After this information is shared, a younger person in the community may come forth and pour libations in honor of the person. Here the youth may state the qualities in the elder that he or she most admires and ways in which he or she hopes to emulate that person's positive example. A libation may be poured after each significant thought or may be poured out at the end of the tribute.

After each tribute, drummers, musicians, or dancers may pay tribute through artistic creativity. The music may be sacred or secular, jazz, spirituals, gospel, blues, reggae, African, or even rhythm and blues. More traditional church music such as hymns or a song by the choir may also be offered. Each church can devise a program of tribute which would be fitting for the personality and contributions of each person honored.

After all the elders are honored and libations have been poured, the elders collectively stand before the entire community and make a statement about their dreams and wishes for the community and its future.

The Offering of Gifts (*Sadaka*)
Designated members of the community may present various gifts or tokens to the elders for their outstanding service. These gifts should symbolize or signify something of meaning or value to the person and embody some important trait of that individual or the significant service he or she has rendered to the community. Keepsakes or gifts of momentous value from Africa may be given to the elder.

The elders respond by presenting a gift of value to a significant young person in the community. Again this gift may be a keepsake or something of value the elder wishes to pass on to the next generation.

Litany of Tribute (*Kusifu*)
The narrator comes before the community and pours libations for the elders. After each pouring, the community members respond.

LEADER: For the great and selfless contributions of our African elders many centuries ago, we raise our humble adulation, adoration, and praise!

PEOPLE: *Ukitazama utaviona!* If you look, you will see them!

LEADER: For the courage, strength, wisdom, energy, intelligence, and endless industry and endurance of our great elders, today we raise our humble adulation, adoration, and praise!

PEOPLE: *Ukitazama utaviona!* If you look, you will see them!

LEADER: Through adversity, suffering, trials, tribulations, sorrows, and pain, the elders have kept their dignity, shared an undying hope, and lived an unwavering faith in God and in the things that are to come. We raise our thanks and praise!

PEOPLE: *Wamesimama! Wamesimama!* They are rising up! They are rising up! They are getting stronger! They are getting stronger!

LEADER: For the strength of community the elders have personified, the joy of service they have exemplified, and the God of truth they have glorified, we raise our thanks and praise!

PEOPLE: *Wamesimama! Wamesimama!* They are rising up! They are rising up!

LEADER: For their progeny and seed and the strength of generations to come in their stead, we raise our thanks and praise!

PEOPLE: *Watu wote na wajue! Watu wote na wajue!* Let all the people know! Let all the people know!

LEADER: For the lives they have touched, the souls they have healed, the waters they have calmed, the storms they

have quelled, the minds they have taught, and the love they
have sealed, we raise our thanks and praise!

PEOPLE: *Watu wote na wajue! Watu wote na wajue!* Let all
the people know! Let all the people know!

ALL: *Wamesimama! Wamesimama!* They are rising up!
They are rising up!

*At this point more music, dance, or other celebrations may be
rendered for the elders.*

Conclusion

The ceremony is concluded in prayer and thanksgiving offered by the minister or an elder in the community.

Funeral Ceremony:
A Celebration of Life

Background

African religions view time as a continuum. This continuum is best described by John Mbiti, who uses two Swahili words—*Sasa* and *Zamani*—to illustrate this concept in relation to life and death. *Sasa* covers the "now" period and has a sense of immediacy, nearness, and "now todayness"; it is a period of immediate concern for the people, since it is where or when we exist. *Zamani* is the period beyond which nothing can go.

> *Zamani* is the graveyard of time, the period of termination, the dimension in which everything finds its halting point. It is the final storehouse for all phenomena and events, the ocean of time in which everything becomes absorbed into reality that is neither after nor before.[1]

Death then is viewed as a process that is not the ending, but a transitional phase within the *Sasa*. At death the individual begins his or her journey to *Zamani*. Reaching *Zamani* means that the memory of all who knew you no longer exists, and your name is no longer called. Name recognition is extremely important because it brings back to the living memories of the departed, such as their personality, love, character, and the important events of their lives. As long as there is someone alive to recall these things, a person remains in the *Sasa*. At the point at which the departed are not remembered by name, perhaps after four or five generations, they move on to the *Zamani*—the end point, the final destination. When they have crossed over to *Zamani,* the process of dying is complete. This Celebration of Life Ceremony views death as a transition. It encourages family and friends to remember the life of the individual and to continue to celebrate that life for generations to come. It helps the departed achieve "personal immortality," which lasts from generation to generation as long as his or her name is called and he or she is remembered. He or she begins the transition to the *Zamani* when his or her descendants no longer remember the person or what he or she stood for.

Participants

- minister
- minister's assistants
- choir
- family members
- friend of the family (optional)

Materials

• two sets of seven candles each

In Advance

• Invite a relative or friend of the family to participate in the pouring of libations.

The Ceremony

Processional

The minister and the minister's assistants lead the processional down the aisle and stand at the head and foot of the coffin as the family views the body and takes their seats in the front pews. The choir in chancel sings a song such as "Siyahamba (We Are Marching in the Light of God)" or "Kumbayah."

Lighting the Passage

Lighting the passage is an opportunity for the young children in the family to participate in the ceremony. Two children and two elders should be chosen to light two sets of seven candles on the altar. The children represent the ones who will learn more about the departed, and the elders represent those who will teach and pass on to the children the life of the one who is now in transition. The minister calls for those who will light with candles the passage for the departed. The number seven represents the seven principles of the *Nguzo Saba*—the seven principles of blackness that are celebrated during Kwanzaa: unity, self-determination, collective work and responsibility, cooperative economics, purpose, creativity, and faith—principles by which all African Americans should live their lives. As the elders pass on the history and important remembrances of the departed, they should always include what that person stood for and what values are important for the children to remember.

MINISTER: I call the youth and the elders of this family to come forward now and light the passage. It is a way we have chosen to symbolize the process of transition, to reaffirm that (*name*) is only continuing a journey that you must assist with. (*Addressing the elders*) Place your hands on the hands of the children as they light the candles. This is your promise to them that you will keep the memory of (*name*) alive by continuing to call (*his/her*) name and sharing your memories and recollections. (*Addressing the children*) As the hands of the elders cover your hands, light these candles, making a commitment to continue the legacy of (*name*). Call (*his/her*) name through words and in reflection. You will be given the responsibility of keeping this name uplifted for as long as you live. You will be given the responsibility of telling your children and your children's children all about (*name*).

As the candles are being lit, a soloist sings a song such as "Don't Cry for Me."

The Closing

MINISTER: We now prepare for the closing. I ask the directors to come forward and arrange the resting place for (*name*).

The minister imparts words of comfort to the family and references scriptures in both the Old and New Testaments.

The Calling

At this point the song "We Shall Behold Him" may be sung and also signed by an individual familiar with sign language. After the song, the obituary is read aloud.

MINISTER: You have called the name of (*name*), and those left behind celebrate (*his/her*) life. We will continue to do so, so (*his/her*) memory shall live on.

Eulogy

The minister gives the eulogy for the departed.

Pouring of Libations

A relative, friend of the family, or member of the pastoral staff comes forward to pour libations to toast the past, present, and future of the family.

LEADER: There is a cherished belief of our ancestors that comforts us through these difficult times—that a person is never dead until he or she is forgotten. The act of pouring libations incorporates this concept that allows us to believe, to remember, to honor, and to cherish memory and life. Pouring libations is a celebration, a paying of homage, a recognition of who we are, where we have come from, and where we are going. Directed by faith and protected by God's grace, I pour libations with the water of the earth because it was from the earth that we came and unto the earth that we will return.

I pour libations to the past. In this family's time of need, I pour libations to (*name of the departed's oldest living female relative*), the matriarch of this family who carries the history of this family and generated the seeds of its growth, faith, and commitment to value, integrity, and the love of children. I pour libations to (*name of the departed's oldest living male relative*), who is the patriarch of this family who has endured the tests of our time and the challenges God has given as a test of faith. The transition of (*name of departed*) was God's answer to us when we asked God to prolong (*his/her*) life on earth. I know you have asked why. I know you have considered your prayers to have gone unanswered. But God did answer your prayers. God simply said no. I pour libations to (*name of the departed and all the person's roles in life, such as mother, wife, daughter, grandmother, and so on*), and above all, God's faithful servant. To the transition you have undertaken, the love, values, and lessons you have left behind, the values you have given, the love you have shown, and the commitment you have given, I pour libations to you, celebrating your transition, knowing you will now and forever more continue to live in the hearts of those who love you.

I pour libations to the present (*insert names of the deceased's children or individuals who represent one generation removed*). (*He/she*) is gone but never forgotten. You must remember the legacy (*he/she*) left for you. Keep (*his/her*) name alive for your children and your children's children.

I pour libations to the future. To (*insert names of the next generation removed*). It is your task to continue to see (*name of the departed*) in your mind, to hear (*his/her*) voice, to smell (*his/her*) fragrance, to know (*him/her*) by (*his/her*) deeds. You are the true keepers of (*his/her*) memory, and you must pass the memory on. *As Salaam Alaikum,* (*name*). Peace be unto you.

The leader pours the libations into a receptacle after each name is called. The water should be discarded outdoors into the ground.

Crossing Over

MINISTER: Our dearly departed (*brother/sister*) has crossed the great spiritual divide. (*He/She*) has made the passage to another place—a place of peace and comfort, a place of joy and eternal tranquillity. (*He/She*) has made (*his/her*) transition in body only, for (*his/her*) spirit still lives among us. A man or woman is not truly dead until his or her name is no longer spoken. (*Deceased's name*)'s name will always be spoken among us in tenderness and respect, with joy, praise, and thanksgiving.

God, we commend to you the soul of our dear (*brother/sister*), (*name*), who has left this earthly abode to move into the pure ethereal realm with you. We look forward to that day when (*he/she*) and all your saints shall rise with you, walk with you, and embody the promises made to those who remain faithfully with you to the end.

We know, God, that this is just the beginning—the genesis of another phase of the journey. Just as the Israelites moved out of Egypt through the wilderness into the promised land, your servant has made the ascent from one station to the next, from one realm to another, from the material earthly mode to the heavenly eternal domain. We thank you for all that (*he/she*) was, all that (*he/she*) left us, and that great truth of (*his/her*) life, which will be the foundation of our continued striving. We give you honor, adoration, and praise for this moment. In the name of Jesus Christ we pray. Amen.

Recessional

The service is turned over to the funeral directors. The recessional song should be a song that is uplifting, but consistent with the occasion, such as "When We All Get to Heaven."

CELEBRATIONS

Celebrations are community-wide ceremonies that occur at specific times throughout the year. They represent historical and religious events, are celebrated by families and/or the entire "village," and foster a sense of family, community, and shared concerns. They include the Kwanzaa Celebration, Kwanzaa Service, The Tools of Freedom Ceremony, Maundy Thursday Service, Good Friday Service, Easter Sunrise Celebration, Mother's Day Celebration, Father's Day Celebration, A Litany of Thanksgiving, and Christmas Celebration.

Kwanzaa Celebration

Background

Kwanzaa is truly a festive occasion. Founded in 1966 by
Dr. Maulana Karenga, Kwanzaa is a celebration of the
first fruits that begins on December 26 and ends on
January 1. According to James C. Anyike, the celebration of Kwanzaa combines elements of our African culture
and African American experience—to provide a framework
for instilling strong values. The word *Kwanzaa* is derived
from the Kiswahili phrase *Matunda ya kwanza,* which means
"first fruits." An extra "a" was added at the end of the word
to distinguish this celebration as an African American holiday.

The African celebration of first fruits of the harvest is
common among many African people. This African practice
is done to thank the Creator for the blessings of food for the
year. The Kwanzaa holiday was created by Dr. Karenga to
reaffirm and restore our African heritage and culture, to introduce the *Nguzo Saba,* to establish a nonhistoric African

American holiday, and to serve as an annual opportunity for us to reaffirm and reinforce our bond as a people.[1]

Kwanzaa is part of the Black Power, Black Pride movement of the sixties. It is a way in which African Americans can celebrate tradition and have a sense of connection which is relevant to our lives as African descendents.

The entire village comes together to celebrate Kwanzaa because it is both a family and community event. The heart of the celebration is the seven principles (*Nguzo Saba*), which are:

- Day 1: *Umoja* or unity
- Day 2: *Kujichagulia* or self-determination
- Day 3: *Ujima* or collective work and responsibility
- Day 4: *Ujamaa* or cooperative economics
- Day 5: *Kuumba* or creativity
- Day 6: *Nia* or purpose
- Day 7: *Imani* or faith

Kwanzaa is an opportunity to discuss and reflect on how we have practiced those principles over the past year and to plan how we will focus on them in the coming year.

Children are an integral part of this celebration and should be featured throughout. The opening celebration should take place before a meal. A potluck, featuring African food, vegetables, and fruit should be included.

The symbols in the village may vary according to the ideas of the committee that puts things together. Planning for Kwanzaa should begin in November and will parallel activities and planning for Christmas.

The suggestions that follow represent a way in which the village can come together and truly understand why the principles of the *Nguzo Saba* are important to African Americans as a people. They create a sense of unity and shared values. Dr. Karenga has discussed procedures for celebrating each day of Kwanzaa. The celebrations described here are part of Kwanzaa activities at Hope United Methodist Church.

Participants

- six parish families, each representing one of the first six principles of Kwanzaa
- minister and family to represent the principle of *Imani*

Materials

- masonite, chicken wire, straw
- gold Mylar paper
- pedestal draped in Kente cloth
- Ashanti stool
- seven tables
- Mylar table cloths (3 red, 3 green, 1 black)
- seven squares of Kente cloth
- *mkeka,* straw mats
- *kinara,* seven candleholders
- *mshumaa saba,* the seven candles (3 red, 1 black, 3 green)
- *muhindi,* ears of corn
- the *kikombe,* the unity cup, and a gourd
- *zawadi,* the gift
- rice, beans, and fruit
- family objects, such as African statues or artwork, pictures of beloved relatives, and so on
- name placards for the seven principles
- traditional African attire for the participants
- gongs or bells
- African music

In Advance

+ Re-create the fellowship hall into an African village, with each item in the village representing a symbol of our African past.

+ Create a replica of an Ibo hut from masonite, chicken wire, and straw. The inside is lined with gold Mylar paper from top to bottom. The hut represents the central focus of our village home. It is both shelter and a connection to the motherland.

+ Place a pedestal draped in Kente cloth inside the door of the hut.

+ Place an Ashanti stool on the pedestal inside the hut. The Ashanti stool is a symbol of solidarity and unity. (According to legend, it was a gift of the supreme deity, Nyame, who descended from above and settled in the lap of the first Ashanti, Osei Tutu. The golden stool embodies the soul of the Ashanti people and serves as a symbol of the divinely inspired solidarity of their nation. Being sacred, the golden stool is never sat upon, but sits on a throne of its own. When Sir Frederick Hodgson, the British governor of the Gold Coast, visited Kumasi, the Ashanti capital, on March 25, 1900, and insisted on sitting on the golden stool, it caused the Queen Mother, Yaa Asantewa, to lead the Ashanti in a rebellion against the British. This rebellion is said to have lasted over thirty years. What a powerful symbol of *Umoja* (unity)!)

+ Set up seven tables at angles to the hut to serve as altars. Place three on each side with the seventh table off center. Each table has a placard and is covered with Mylar paper. Use red covers for *Umoja, Kujichagulia,* and *Ujima;* green for *Ujamaa, Kuumba,* and *Nia;* and black for *Imani.*

A yard of Kente cloth is centered on each table, and each family is asked to bring in their Kwanzaa altar items and decorate their tables. These may include a *mkeka* or straw mat; the *kinara,* a candleholder that holds seven candles; *mshumaa saba,* the seven candles with a black candle in the center, three red candles to the right, and three green candles to the left; *muhindi,* ears of corn to represent each child in the family and/or the desire for a child; the *kikombe,* or unity cup; and the *zawadi,* or gift.

- Sprinkle rice and beans on each table and add a bowl of fruit to represent the "first fruit."
- Encourage families to bring African statues or artwork, pictures of beloved relatives, and so on, to decorate their tables.
- If possible, keep the hall out of view until the celebration begins.
- Encourage everyone, including the children, to dress in African attire to represent a connection with the mother country and to show the regal elegance of our history as kings and queens.

The Ceremony

The Village Is Called

The more dramatically this part of the ceremony can be presented, the better. Everyone should be seated in a darkened hall. The gongs or bells are sounded, and African music is played as everyone is seated. Then the mistress or master of ceremonies welcomes everyone to the celebration of the first fruits and explains the symbolism of the re-created village and the importance of our extended families coming together as a "welcome to our village."

The Pouring of Libations

One of the men of the village is called upon to pour libations. He toasts the past, paying homage to past members of the church, the church's history, and to those whose names we cannot call. He pours a little water from a *kikombe* into a gourd.

VILLAGE: *N'sah.*

The participant then pours a libation to the present, naming key leaders of the church and community and naming the families who will participate in the celebration. He pours a little of the water from the kikombe *into a gourd.*

VILLAGE: *N'sah.*

Finally, he pours a libation to the future, toasting the children in the church and village and those yet to come. He pours a little of the water from the kikombe *into a gourd.*

VILLAGE: *N'sah.*

He then calls the men of the village to come forward. Ten preselected men should come forward and stand in a horseshoe shape. The man pouring libations then calls the minister to come forward as the leader of the village. He passes the kikombe *to the minister, saying: As the leader of the village, the minister is the most worthy to take the first drink from the cup.*

The Proclamation

The minister briefly talks about the responsibility of leadership and the role of the men in the village, ending by saying: I am honored to receive this cup, but you, my brother, are most worthy.

The minister passes the *kikombe* to the next man without taking a drink. He then moves to stand next to the man at the opposite end of the horseshoe.

Each man in turn takes the *kikombe* and states: I, too, am honored (*explaining briefly why before turning to the next man and saying*): I am worthy, but you, my brother, are the most worthy.

Each man in turn speaks and passes the cup on. This continues until each man has passed the *kikombe* (without drinking from it) and it is returned to the minister at the end of the line.

MINISTER (raising the *kikombe*): As the leader of this village and on behalf of the men of this village, I drink from this cup.

At this point, the minister takes the only drink and returns the kikombe *and gourd to the* Imani *table. The water in the gourd is poured outside onto the ground after the celebration.*

Nguzo Saba
Children who have spent time studying Kwanzaa and have a very good understanding of its principles perform a presentation through a song, dance, skit, poetry reading, or story that reflects the children's understanding of the Kwanzaa principles.

Habari Gani? (What Is the News?)
The families are called to take their places behind their tables. Each family, in turn, is asked: *Habari gani*, what is the news? What is your message to this village?

Each family says something profound, with an explanation of the principle that they represent. After making their statement, each family lights the appropriate candle. After the minister's family presents *Imani,* the minister lights the black candle. All the other families follow. The room lights are dimmed. Everyone lights the appropriate candle together after each principle is described.

Sankofa

As African music is played softly in the background, the minister briefly discusses where we have come from as a people and charges everyone to practice the concepts of the *Nguzo Saba* over the next year. The African music increases in volume.

MINISTER (*concluding the celebration*): *Wa salaam alaikum* (Peace be unto you)!

VILLAGE: *Wa alaikum salaam.*

Ideas for celebrating for the remainder of the week include:

- a dinner each night at the church.
- a home fellowship in which several families agree to host a potluck at their homes and members of the congregation sign up to attend (the host families should put together a program based on the principle of the day of their meal).
- a worship service related to Kwanzaa, such as the ceremony that follows

Kwanzaa Service:
A Celebration of First Fruits and
Recognition of the *Nguzo Saba*

Background

This is an opportunity to bring the celebration of Kwanzaa into the worship service. It represents a celebration of the harvesting of the first fruits in recognition of the work and labor that have gone into the blessings we are now receiving. Many modern-day congregations do not include farmers, and the people do not literally harvest grains, fruits, and vegetables. We are all, however, laborers. Whether we work in factories, on farms, in schools, in our homes, or in corporations and businesses, our work affords us the opportunity to receive first fruits. This ceremony, then, becomes a way to reflect on our blessings from God over the last year. We can use this opportunity to tithe—to give back to God in thanksgiving for God's blessings—and to maintain or begin a tradition of first fruits.

It is recommended that the Kwanzaa ceremony be conducted during the offertory. Instead of passing the offertory plates, the congregation will be asked to bring their offering or "first fruits" of the new year to the altar. They will be asked to reflect on how they practiced the principles of the *Nguzo Saba* over the last year and how they intend to continue to uphold these principles during the coming year. This ceremony is designed around the concepts of *Sankofa* and the pouring of libations.

Participants

- minister
- acolytes

Materials

- a traditional table
- *mkeka,* a straw mat
- *kinara,* a candleholder
- *mshumaa saba,* the seven candles
- *muhindi,* ears of corn
- *kikombe,* the unity cup
- *zawadi,* the gift
- a bowl of fresh fruit
- a bright, festive table cover
- ornate banners, cloths, or table runners depicting the seven principles of the *Nguzo Saba*
- a large, ornately decorated basket for offerings
- music

In Advance

- Prepare a traditional table with a bright, festive cover near the altar to display the *mkeka, kinara, mshumaa saba, muhindi, kikombe,* and *zawadi.*
- A bowl of fresh fruit should be placed on or near the altar.
- The seven principles of the *Nguzo Saba* should be displayed in an ornate fashion in the sanctuary, as banners, cloths on the table, or runners.
- A large, ornately decorated basket should be available for the congregation to place their offerings in.

Scripture Reading

As part of our heritage and in keeping with tradition, we give thanks to the Creator for the blessings of food and God's many gifts for the year. According to 2 Thessalonians 2:15, "Therefore, brethren, stand fast, and hold the traditions which ye have been taught, whether by word, or our epistle."

The Ceremony

The minister and the acolytes step behind the table and face the congregation. The acolytes light their candlelighters from the altar candles and stand on each side of the minister.

MINISTER: We light the candles representing the seven principles of the *Nguzo Saba,* welcoming the new year, thanking God for our blessings, and affirming the principles that guide our lives. Renewed in the acceptance of our heritage, we light the candles representing this, our first fruits celebrations.

The pastor says a few short words about each principle— Umoja, *unity;* Kujichagulia, *self-determination;* Ujima, *collective work and responsibility;* Ujamaa, *cooperative economics;* Kuumba, *creativity;* Nia, *purpose;* Imani, *faith—as the acolytes light each candle in turn. They should alternately light red and green candles. The last candle to be lit will be the black candle in the middle.*

Libations

The minister raises the *kikombe* and pours libations, toasting the past, present, and future.

MINISTER: I pour libations to the past, paying homage to the traditions of our people and to every first harvest representing the gifts from our savior Jesus Christ. I pour libations to the present; to our children so they will know not only who they are but whose they are; for our children to render unto Caesar the things that are Caesar's and unto God the things that are God's. I pour libations to the future; for all of us to have a bountiful harvest, remembering that all glory belongs to God!

The Offering

MINISTER (*to the congregation*): Now come forward.

> Will a man rob God? Yet ye have robbed me. But ye say, Wherein have we robbed thee? In tithes and offerings. Bring ye all the tithes into the storehouse, that there may be meat in mine house, and prove me now herewith, saith the Lord of hosts, if I will not open you the windows of heaven, and pour you out a blessing, that there shall not be room enough to receive it. (Malachi 3:8, 10)

The members of the congregation are directed to walk down the center aisle to deposit their offering (first fruit) in the basket as appropriate upbeat music plays. After the last offering has been deposited, the minister lifts the basket and blesses the first fruits.

The Tools of Freedom Ceremony:
A Celebration of the Emancipation Proclamation and a Salute to Black Heroes

We hold these truths to be self-evident, that all [people] are created equal, that they are endowed by their Creator with certain unalienable Rights, that among these are Life, Liberty, and the pursuit of Happiness.

—THE DECLARATION OF INDEPENDENCE

Background

This ceremony involves bringing back to life the black heroes of African American history to discuss, from their perspective, the pursuit of freedom, equality, and justice. It also affirms the concept that freedom is costly and that the tools of freedom are many and varied.

The best setting for this ceremony would be a church. It may be presented as part of a service or as a special program. The members of the congregation will be taken by surprise as the characters, seated among them, rise from their seats and move up the aisles to take their place on the altar or in a strategic place in the church that will add drama to the presentation.

The characters described here are only a few of hundreds of black heroes. We strongly encourage you to personalize the ceremony by adding new heroes or substituting other heroes for those who are presented here.

Participants

- ◆ Biddy Mason
- ◆ Gracia
- ◆ Harriet Tubman
- ◆ Frederick Augustus Washington Bailey
- ◆ Dred Scott
- ◆ Martin Luther King
- ◆ "Negro Ensemble" of singers

Materials

- ◆ audio equipment
- ◆ period clothing for participants

In Advance

- ◆ Secretly assign roles to members of the congregation and allow time for them to rehearse their parts.
- ◆ Have the participants, dressed in appropriate period clothing for the characters they represent, sit inconspicu-

ously in the congregation, scattered around the front, back, and sides of the sanctuary.

* Choose members for the a capella "Negro Ensemble" to sing throughout the ceremony. The ensemble should include no more than sixteen people, with four singers assigned to each part: soprano, alto, tenor, and bass. Keeping the group small allows them to pose and move about, singing from different positions and moving throughout the congregation.

* Provide period clothing for the "Negro Ensemble." For example, the men may wear tattered clothing, with frayed pants held up by a rope, and straw hats. The women may wear long dresses, white aprons, and head scarves.

* Select appropriate songs, such as the Negro spirituals "Every Time I Feel the Spirit," "Chariots Comin'," and "Wade in the Water," and have the ensemble rehearse the songs.

* The placement of audio equipment should be planned ahead of time, making sure the characters are miked so they can be heard even before they are seen.

The Ceremony

The minister comes to the pulpit so the congregation will focus their attention on the minister. The minister begins discussing the Emancipation Proclamation and its importance to black history. He or she talks about the concept of freedom, what freedom means, the price of freedom, and the importance of freedom. The minister speaks for five to ten minutes before giving the cue that will be interrupted by the first character.

MINISTER: . . . the tools of freedom come from the resources of the hour. They must be forged out of necessity,
dreams, desires and determination . . .

BIDDY MASON (*standing up near the rear of the church and
calling out*): Excuse *me,* Pastor, excuse *me.* I know the price
of freedom. A lot of ya'll may not know me, but my name
is Biddy Mason, and I be from Mississippi. In 1848 there
was a major gold rush in California. My masta wanted to
find him a fortune in gold and he took me, my family, and
other slaves from Mississippi to California. I walked, and
my job was to keep the cattle together. I walked across the
country, so I know the price of freedom. I remember I was
thirty-two years old when us first made this trip. When us
got to California it was 'mazing that they didn't want
Negroes, Chinese, Mexicans, Injuns, and Spaniards to work
in the gold mines. In fact, they said that Negroes had some
special power to find gold. They went as far as to kill off
slaves that worked in the mines. They killed a number of
slaves, told the slave owners, "Remove yo' slaves or face the
consequences." Some Negroes did mine tho', and some
saved enough money to buy they freedom, but you know
them sly white devils took they gold and wouldn't keep
they word to free the slaves. But the slaves they kept tryin',
minin', and payin', and some of them did buy they freedom. While I still be responsible for the cattle, Masta had a
number of slaves that worked in them gold mines in
California, but then one day the masta he said that we was
all goin' to return to Mississippi and that we had to walk.
Well, I wasn't gonna go back to Mississippi, and I couldn't
see my daughters livin' that kind of life—especially when I

knew and understood that freedom was possible. So I went to work and in time—I worked hard, I worked the gold mine, I made friends, and finally—with the aid of the local sheriff, I won my freedom and the freedom of my three girls and us stayed in California. Us didn't have to make that walk back to slavery, and poverty, and indignity. Us stayed right here in California. I stayed, and we was among some of the lucky ones that remained there, and we lived a free life in California. In fact, I felt it was my responsibility to sort of help all them Negroes, free and slave. I bought land because land is our roots, our piece of the earth. Land is important 'cause that's where we came from and that's where we gonna return. I had enough land and I was soon able to give land to schools, churches, and hospitals. Yeah, I know the cost of freedom; the cost of freedom is a walk from Mississippi to California.

You call my name; my name is Biddy Mason. Ya'll may not know me, but call my name.

Biddy is moving to the front of the church, talking and interacting along the way. Once she reaches the front and completes her speech, she freezes in place. The Negro Ensemble sings: "Oh Freedom, Deep River, Free At Last" or "Keep Your Lights Trimmed and Burning."

GRACIA (rising from the congregation): Biddy Mason, I know what you mean. My name is Gracia and I date from a long time ago, and nobody here may know who I am either because I fought the United States. I lived in the Spanish province of Florida. I helped repel the invasion of the Americans. We lived among the Seminoles and the Creeks.

The Injuns were our friends. They took us in, and they fought beside us. When word came that the Americans were about to invade the Spanish province of Florida, we worked together 'cause they couldn't do that. Them Americans took Injun land and Negro freedom. There was a fort there in Florida, and the fort was called Fort Negro; we lived there on the Apalachicola River. There was hundreds of us men, women, and children living in that fort, and I was in charge. Fort Negro meant freedom. But them Americans knew that southern blacks were running away and joining us. Fort Negro represented freedom, and for some reason them Americans felt it had to be destroyed (*laughs sarcastically*). Andrew Jackson, he ordered them soldiers to destroy Fort Negro and give the Negroes who lived there back to their masters. Our very existence could not be tolerated 'cause we weren't suppose to be able to live, survive, and prosper on our own. They said we needed the white masters to tell us what to do. They said we would die without 'em. They said they had to get rid of us 'fore too many slaves realized they could live—and live well—as free people. We opened our fort to all Negroes who could make it there.

In the background, the ensemble softly sings "Don't You Let Nobody Turn You 'Roun'."

GRACIA: Here we was, free and proud people, armed and dangerous, friends of the Seminoles and the Creeks. We had to go. Them Spaniards soon sold Florida to the Americans, and they came and they attacked in the summer of 1816. They stood outside Fort Negro, and they said that we had to surrender. I told them, "Shoot your best shot

'cause we ain't coming out." They attacked. On July 27
them gunboats attacked Fort Negro—cannonballs bounced
off the walls of the fort and landed in the mud—then you
know what they did? They heated up them there cannon
balls red hot and one of 'em landed inside the fort on our
ammo. Lucky shot! It just blew up and killed just about
everybody—men, women, and the chillens—not many survived. But we fought. We fought, I tell you. They killed me
in front of a firing squad. The others that survived were
taken back to Georgia, to slavery. We kept fighting. It was a
call to arms. But resistance didn't end that July 27 because
other Negroes and Seminoles they resisted to the end.
Them Americans had to fight the Seminoles. I heard say it
cost them Americans a lot, and them wars didn't end 'til
'bout the 1840s. One of them generals admitted they were
fighting Negroes, not them Injuns, 'cause to let them
Negroes live free in Florida could mean a heavy toll on slavery. Our tools for freedom was simple—we lived well and
prospered—I guess that was our best revenge.

*Gracia takes his place in front and freezes in position. The en-
semble sings the Negro spiritual "Sometimes I Feel Like a
Motherless Child," "Swing Low, Sweet Chariot," or "I'm So
Glad Trouble Don't Last Always."*

HARRIET TUBMAN (*rising*): It is amazing to me how, as I
look over these times, we are still talking about freedom.
Some of ya may know me, and some of ya may not—my
name is Harriet Tubman, and I was born in 1820. I guess I
died in 1913. I escaped from slavery in Maryland by using
a tool of freedom, the best tool anybody could ever have—

my feet. I followed the north star in the sky and found my
way to Philadelphia. Whilst I was there, I joined the
Underground Railroad. I felt that it was my responsibility
to help and put the tool of freedom to work. If my feet
made me free, then others could use their feet to do the
same thing. I walked that ground over nineteen times to
walk my family to freedom. I musta walked over six hundred feets to freedom through this here Underground
Railroad. I had one rule, and the rule was simple—the passage was one way. If you didn't continue, you died where
you stood. Knew too much, too much at stake, we walked
for freedom. I used that freedom tool to free many, many
slaves, to take them through the Underground Railroad.
Stations was set up from South to North, from North to
Canada. We used secret words that went with the railroad
so slaves would know who to talk to to find underground
houses and people to shelter them. Many ya'll probably
thought that the Underground Railroad was mostly white
folks who took pity on black folks, or Christians who felt
slavery was not Godlike; that ain't true (*almost angrily*).
Many Negroes, we worked hard to make sure that others
were able to walk to freedom. You know when we stopped
that Underground Railroad? Right up 'til they signed that
Emancipation Proclamation thang. Right up 'til they abol-
ished slavery. Cause we didn't trust 'em. We was ready to
walk for a long time after that. You know what? I had to
find me another job so I became a Union spy (*laughs*). I
guess you could say I was one of the first CIA agents
(*smiles*). I had me a network of slaves behind Southern
lines. They underestimated us. Guess they thought we

couldn't hear or see, let alone think. Well, finally my feet got tired, and I walked that last time as a free woman.

The ensemble sings the Negro spiritual "This Train" or "Go Down Moses."

FREDERICK AUGUSTUS WASHINGTON BAILEY (*loudly, from his seat in the congregation*): "Wake the black man from his slumber / let him see this mighty sight. / Watchman speak and tell my people / what's the hour of the night?" I suppose a lot of folks know me because I used my mouth and my mind as tools of freedom. Harriet, I love you. (*Harriet acknowledges him.*) Yes, my name is Frederick Augustus Washington Bailey. I changed my name to Frederick Douglas in 1841. I'm not quite sure when I was born. I think I was born about 1817. My quest for freedom included learning how to read. In fact, that was the most powerful thing I could have done. I remember . . .

> I went to live with Mr. and Mrs. Auld; she was very kindly and she commenced to teach me the ABCs. And after I had learned this, she assisted me in learning to spell words with three or four letters. Just at this point in my progress, Mr. Auld found out what was going on and at once forbade Mrs. Auld to instruct me further, telling her, among other things, that it was unlawful as well as unsafe to teach a slave to read. To use his own words he said, "If you give a nigger an inch, he will take an ell. A nigger should know nothing but to obey his master, to do as he is told to do. Learning will spoil the best nigger in the world," said he. "If you teach that nigger," speaking of myself and pointing, "how to read,

there will be no peace. It will forever unfit him to be a slave. He will have at once become unmanageable and of no value to his master or to himself. It could do him no good but a great deal of harm. It would make him discontented and unhappy."

These words sank into my heart, stirred up sentiments that had laid in slumber and called into existence an entirely new train of thought. It was a new and special revelation explaining dark and mysterious things without which my youthful understanding would have been to me a more complexing difficulty, to wit the white men's power to enslave the black man. It was a grand achievement and I prized it highly. From that moment, I understood the pathway from slavery to freedom. It was just what I wanted; I got it at a time when I was least expecting it. Whilst I was saddened by the thought of losing the aid of my kind mistress, I was gladdened by the invaluable instruction which, by the merest accident, I had gained from my master. Though conscious of the difficulty of learning without a teacher, I set out with a high hope and a fixed hope and at whatever cost or trouble to learn how to read.[1]

It took me four long years, but I learned, and I know that to me this was the valuable price of freedom. I hear it again now: "You teach that nigger to read, and there'll be no keeping him." He was right, because when I learned how to read there was no keeping me! That was the tool I used—it was reading. It's important that we use these tools—all the tools—to continue the struggle.

Believing that one of the best means of emancipating the slaves of the South is to improve and elevate the characters of the free colored people of the North, I shall labor in the future, as I have labored in the past, to promote the moral, social, religious, and intellectual elevation of the free colored people; never forgetting my own humble origin, nor refusing, while Heaven leads my ability, to use my voice, my pen, or my vote, to advocate the great and primary work of the universal and unconditional emancipation of my entire race.[2]

You must always use the tools of freedom, whether it's your feet, whether it's the power of the word, or whether it's the struggle.

There is a brief period of silence. Finally Dred Scott stands near the front of the church, hat in hand.

DRED SCOTT: And now looking over the history books, many folks describe me as listless and a slave that didn't even know what was happening to him. Yeah, some of ya'll may know me; my name is Dred Scott. Just 'member that my tool for freedom was persistence. A lot of folks looked at me as an ignorant person. I don't be ignorant; I knew that what was important was important. I had purpose. For over ten years and ten months, I pressed my case for freedom for me and my family through the court of the United States. Seems to me since me and my family had lived on free land, we should be free. Simple truth made sense to me and a lot of folks. If they changed the law, it would help lots of slaves, but you won't believe this: the United States Supreme

Court said no. They said that me and my family was not entitled to freedom (*shaking head, disgusted*). I don't know, but you know there was this young whippersnapper, ugly cuss, his name, uh . . . let me recall his name . . . it's been so long, but I think you might know him; his name was Abraham Lincoln, and he was one of them new Republicans. He made the most of this case; his platform, as you call it now, was anti-slavery. Republican guy. Lots of folks joined up. Anti-slavery grew, and three years later they elected that boy president of the United States. He was responsible for that Emancipation Proclamation. My persistence made his point and gave you yo' freedom.

The ensemble sings the Negro spiritual "There's a Meeting Here Tonight" or "Going to Hold Out to the End."

MARTIN LUTHER KING (*rising*): My tools for freedom? I had several. One was a dream; I had a dream. Another was tension. And another was confronting and using the tools of the time to get the message across.

A dream represents what could be. Without a dream or a vision, we just live day to day and accept the things we feel we cannot change. We had to share the dream through nonviolent tension—we made people see that this is not the way, that this is not the kind of America we wanted to live in. We had to teach old Bull Connor his lesson. In full view of the world, he learned a lesson—he learned a lesson because as I told the nation,

> He got his dogs, but it wasn't long before Bull Connor discovered that we had something within that dogs couldn't bite. He got his fire hoses, but it wasn't long after that he discovered we had a fire shut up in our

bones that water couldn't put out. He got his paddy wagons, but it was long after that he discovered that we had numbers that paddy wagons couldn't hold. He took us to his jails and it wasn't long after that before he called the city jail of Birmingham, the County Jail, the Bessemer Jail, and the Bessemer Fairgrounds and they were all filled up with Negroes and there was 2000 more ready to go to jail.[3]

My tool of freedom involved the tools that everybody has talked about here today—our feet to march to freedom, our persistence, our determination, our ability to read and to write, our ability to use those tools because freedom for all intents and purposes is not free—it cost many lives and will continue to do so until we are all free, socially, economically, politically, and physically. We must use all the tools of freedom—the vote, education, persistence, the willingness to always work toward justice, freedom, and equality. Now is not the time to sleep.

The ensemble sings the Negro spiritual "Don't You Let Nobody Turn You 'Roun'."

Declaration of Freedom

Martin Luther King takes his place near the altar in the center of all the characters that have come forward out of the congregation, and the minister begins to talk more about freedom, the tools of freedom, and the importance of freedom. It is important that the minister put these ideas in his or her own words to help the congregation understand the here and now—the things that are important now and the needs based on the times of this presentation. Afterward, the minister comes down in front of the characters from history who are on the stage to pour libations.

Sankofa

MINISTER: In order to know where we are going we have to know where we have come from. And for each of you standing there, I lift this cup, knowing that a person is never dead until he or she is forgotten. I call your names.

Libations

MINISTER: I pour libations to Biddy Mason, whose tools of freedom were the understanding that freedom was possible and her caring and giving heart.

I pour libations to Gracia, who never surrendered and whose tool of freedom was living well and prospering.

I pour libations to Harriet Tubman, who said this ticket is a one-way fare; either you keep going or die where you stand—whose tool of freedom was her feet.

I pour libations to Frederick Augustus Washington Bailey, who learned that if you taught a "nigger" to read, there'd be no keeping him and then—after four long years—learned to read!

I pour libations to Dred Scott for his persistence and for paving the way for the Emancipation Proclamation.

I pour libations to Martin Luther King, who had a dream—the dream and the vision of what we all must continue to strive to be.

I pour libations to each of you whose responsibility it is to use ceaselessly the tools of freedom.

Closing

The ceremony ends with the singing of the African American national anthem, "Lift Every Voice and Sing."

Maundy Thursday Service

Background

Maundy Thursday is essentially a day of preparation. It marks a major transition in the holiest of events of Christian faith. It is included here as a ceremony to help Christians feel the feelings Christ must have been experiencing the day before he died. The prophecy was unfolding before his eyes, and he had to prepare himself for his own death.

This ceremony is a solemn occasion and should pull at the emotions of everyone present. The entire village attends this ceremony in silence so they can truly reflect on the powerful meaning of this day. Hope United Methodist Church began this annual ceremony around 1990, and it has evolved over the years. It involves singing, praying, dancing, and sound effects that can transport you to the "Upper Room" to experience the Last Supper.

The ceremony can be held in any place that can host a large gathering and meal, such as a fellowship hall, a rental hall, a hotel banquet room, or any other banquet facility. The hall should be darkened and tables should be set up with black tablecloths and votive candles centered in grape vine wreaths that represent a crown of thorns. Black plates and eating utensils should be used. Three large wooden crosses are placed near the front of the room, off to the side, and the middle cross, draped in black, must be larger than the other two. Place some decorations around the base of the cross to depict a hill and light the crosses with a very soft light. Solos and songs should be sung in front of this setting. At the front of the room is a U-shaped table where Jesus and the disciples are seated; behind the table is an elevated stage.

The key to this ceremony is the silence from the audience. It is important that everyone understands what will happen and why. Children are welcome, but parents should speak to them and share as much of what they will experience as possible by telling them the story of the Last Supper.

Participants

+ thirteen volunteers to take the roles of Jesus and the twelve disciples
+ narrator
+ angels
+ choir

Materials

+ tables
+ black table cloths
+ votive candles arranged in grape vine wreaths

- black plates and eating utensils
- three large wooden crosses, one larger than the others
- a black drape
- costumes for actors
- ingredients for the Paschal meal, including roast lamb (Pascal lamb), matzos (unleavened bread), lehus (horse-radish), bitter herbs, Passover wine, rice, olives, figs, dates, oranges
- sacred or secular music that is very provocative, meaningful, and sad
- recording of "Strange Fruits"
- programs
- gong
- tape of storm sounds
- incense

In Advance

- Prepare the hall.
- Prepare the Paschal meal.
- Provide time for participants to rehearse.
- Prepare printed programs.

The Ceremony

Sankofa

As people gather, they should not enter the hall but should remain in the foyer, sanctuary, or some other area. They may talk in this area in hushed tones. The programs can be distributed at this time so people will know what to expect. Fifteen minutes before the door is opened, the leader of the village greets everyone.

MINISTER: We are gathered here to feel the feeling of our savior Jesus Christ. It is the foundation of our beliefs that on Good Friday he will die and on Easter he will rise from the dead. Who we are as Christians is founded in the events of the next three days. Tonight is his last supper. Imagine what it was like to know that the people you most trusted in the world will not be there for you and that one will actually betray you. Your most trusted friends will deny you. We are asking you tonight to feel the feeling, knowing that tomorrow Jesus will die a painful and agonizing death. Pontius Pilate will find no fault with this man. The events of the evening will be reenacted for you so you may listen, hear, and, above all, feel.

When the gong rings three times, the door to the Upper Room will open. Once you cross the threshold of the Upper Room, you should not speak until you leave this place.

The Village Is Called

A gong or the church bells ring three times. The doors to the Upper Room are opened. As the villagers file to their seats, the background sound effects of a quiet storm should fill the room. Incense, such as sandalwood or another earthy scent, may be burned. The visual effects of the room should be striking. Once everyone is seated, the soloist, dressed in black, sings "Calvary."

Jesus and Two Disciples Enter

Two actors, representing Peter and John, are dressed in the clothing of the era or in African attire and are talking quietly. NARRATOR: Now the Feast of Unleavened Bread, called the Passover, was approaching, and the Chief Priests and the

Teachers of the law were looking for some way to get rid of Jesus, for they were afraid of the people. Then Satan entered Judas, called Iscariot, one of the twelve, and Judas went to the Chief Priests and the officers of the temple guard and discussed with them how he might betray Jesus. They were delighted and agreed to give him money. He consented and watched for an opportunity to hand Jesus over to them when no crowd was present. Then came the Day of Unleavened Bread on which the Passover lamb had to be sacrificed (Luke 22:1–6).

Jesus enters the room opposite the crosses.

JESUS: Peter, John—go and make preparations for us to eat the Passover meal.

JOHN: When do you want us to prepare for it?

JESUS: As you enter the city, a man carrying a jar of water will meet you. Follow him to the house that he enters and say to the owner of the house, "The Teacher asks, 'Where is the guest room where I may eat the Passover meal with my disciples?'" He will show you a large upper room all furnished. Make preparations there.

NARRATOR: They left and found things just as Jesus had told them. So they prepared the Passover.

All the disciples enter, talking quietly among themselves, and take a seat at the head table. Jesus is seated in the middle.

The Pascal Meal Is Served to Everyone

As the choir sings "Surely He Hath Borne Our Griefs," the village eats in silence. The disciples are engaging in quiet conversation. Judas is at the end of the table, looking nervous and fidgety—obviously looking around, looking out of the windows if there are any. Jesus glances his way several times throughout the course of the meal. After everyone is served and about fifteen minutes into the meal, a small choir sings "Judas, Mercator Pessimus" and "The Lamb of God Behold." The disciples complete their meal, and their table is cleared. The sacraments should already be on each table.

Communion

NARRATOR: Jesus is obviously troubled, and the disciples appear to be a bit perplexed by his behavior. Can you imagine the struggle that Jesus must have been going through? To know that one among the men he most trusted in the world would betray him! How could this be after three long years? Tomorrow he will be delivered to be crucified. Tomorrow he will die. When the hour came, Jesus and his apostles relaxed at the table.

JESUS (*standing*): I have eagerly desired to eat this Passover meal with you before I suffer. For I tell you, I will not eat it again until it finds fulfillment in the Realm of God.

The disciples look perplexed and whisper among themselves, curious about what Jesus may mean.

JESUS (*picking up the bread*): Take and eat for this is my body which is given to you—do this in remembrance of me (Luke 22:19).

NARRATOR: After the same manner, also he took the cup and when he had drunk it, he said:

JESUS: Drink ye all of this, for this is my blood which is shed for you for the remission of sins. This do as oft as ye drink it in remembrance of me.

The choir sings "Agnus Dei." Jesus walks behind the disciples, who appear very supportive and are confirming what he is saying. Jesus should talk about all the times they have shared and how the scriptures must come to pass. He puts his hands on each of their shoulders as he walks behind them.

JESUS (*moving behind Judas*): But the hand of he who is going to betray me is with mine on the table. The son of man will go as it has been decreed, but woe to that man who betrays him.

JUDAS (*jumping up in panic*): Jesus, how could you say something like that? We are your disciples, and we would never betray you. We love you. I am with you; I'll always be with you.

Judas gives Jesus a hug and a kiss and runs from the room. The other disciples jump up, speaking all at once. They are talking to themselves and asking Jesus individually if they will betray him. Jesus moves the group to the exit door, and all the disciples leave the room. Jesus is behind the group, with Peter behind him. Before Jesus exits the room Peter calls him back.

SIMON PETER: Jesus, it can't be me. I am ready to go with you to prison and to death.

JESUS: I tell you, Peter, that before the rooster crows, you will deny me three times.

Sound effects come up, and the introduction to the tape "Strange Fruits" is played. Judas is on stage. The curtain opens slowly, and there is a hangman's noose center stage. Judas dances to the song "Strange Fruits." The ending of the dance is a simulation of Judas hanging himself. As he falls to the floor, the curtains close. The wind and storm sound effects go on until the angels are in place on stage. They are in place when Jesus and the disciples return to the scene.

NARRATOR: The hour was fast approaching, and Jesus went with his disciples as usual to the Mount of Olives. On reaching the place he said to them:

JESUS: Watch and pray with me. I have need of your support.

Leaving the disciples on one side of the stage, Jesus crosses to the opposite side and kneels to pray.

NARRATOR: Jesus withdrew about a stone's throw beyond them, knelt down, and prayed. The disciples settled themselves and soon found themselves fast asleep. In the garden, Jesus is alone and frightened. He prays.

JESUS: God, if it is your will, take this bitter cup from me; yet not my will but thine be done.

NARRATOR: Jesus prayed and the disciples slept. Then God sent angels from heaven and strengthened him.

Have the choir sing or play a recording of "We Shall Behold Him." The song is signed by children dressed as angels. They appear on stage behind Jesus as he prays. When the song ends, the curtain closes. The sound effects of the wind and thunderstorm play for at least two minutes. Jesus walks across the stage and wakens the disciples, and they exit the room. The storm continues and the gong rings three times, signaling the congregation to depart. The doors open and everyone is escorted out of the hall. All should maintain silence until they are in their cars.

Good Friday Ceremony:
The Seven Last Words

Background

This ceremony can be a continuation of the Maundy Thursday ceremony. It serves as a vivid reminder of the agony Jesus endured for our sins. It is a provocative way to get everyone involved and to feel the feeling. The majority of the narrative is taken from the books of Matthew, Mark, Luke, and John.

The recommended setting for this ceremony is the church sanctuary. The crosses that were used on Maundy Thursday should be brought into the sanctuary and placed on the altar or in front of the church. A sheer tearaway curtain should be hung behind the crosses. It will be torn in half at the end of the service. The center cross should be draped with the black cloth. A sign that says "Jesus of Nazareth, The King of the Jews" should hang in the sanctuary. It may be printed in Ki-swahili,

Aramaic, Latin, Greek, or English. The lighting is focused on the crosses, while the remainder of the sanctuary is darkened. A backless chair is placed in front of the church on the floor. Once everyone is seated, the doors are closed and no one is allowed entry after the service starts.

Participants

◆ volunteers to take the roles of Jesus and disciples, Mary, a woman, first man, second man, Pontius Pilate
◆ narrator
◆ choir

Materials

◆ three large wooden crosses, one larger than the others
◆ a black drape
◆ a sheer, easily torn curtain
◆ sacred or secular music that is very provocative, meaningful, and sad
◆ poster board
◆ tape of storm sounds
◆ tape of rooster crowing three times
◆ costumes for actors, including purple *buba* for Jesus

In Advance

◆ Prepare the stage.
◆ Print the sign.
◆ Provide time for participants to rehearse.

The Ceremony

The storm sound effects are playing as the people enter and take their seats. Once again people are asked to remain silent and pray as they remain in their seats throughout the program. A choir, dressed in black, is in the chancel and about twenty participants are seated throughout the front half of the church. The disciples are standing off to the sides near the front looking lost, frustrated, angry, and, above all, helpless. Mary, the mother of Jesus, should be seated on the front row along with the disciple John. A soloist rises and sings "There Is a Green Hill Far Away." Storm sound effects are loud and persistent. Above the storm, we hear the voice of Jesus speaking powerfully and remorsefully.

JESUS: As it is written in Psalm 42:7–9, all my enemies whispered against me; they imagined the worst for me, saying, "A vile disease has beset him; he will never get up from the place where he lies." Even my close friend whom I trusted, he who shared my bread, has lifted up his heel against me.

Peter enters a side door and a woman near the front rises.

WOMAN: Hey! Aren't you the one that followed Jesus?
PETER: Woman, I don't know him!

The actors are silent as the storm rages. A few minutes pass while Peter wanders around nervously. A man stands up as Peter passes.

FIRST MAN: You are one of them!
PETER: Man, I am not!

Peter takes a seat in front of the church, sitting on the steps of the altar. He is trying to cover himself and looking around carefully. Another man stands up and runs up to him.

SECOND MAN: Certainly this fellow was with him, for he is a Galilean.
PETER: Man, I don't know what you are talking about.

Just as Peter is speaking a rooster crows three times above the storm. Peter runs from the sanctuary. As the storm continues, the narrator takes Peter's place on the altar.

NARRATOR: Sit with me. Watch and pray. For the hour comes that the Savior shall give his life so that you may live. Sit with me. Watch and pray. Is it not written in Isaiah 53:8 that by oppression and judgment he was taken away? And who spoke of his descendants? For he was cut off from the land of the living; for the transgression of my people he was stricken.

The storm rages on, and there is commotion in the back of the church as Jesus is led down the aisle with his hands tied in front of him, stumbling along the way. Jesus should be dressed in a purple grand buba. *Soldiers are leading him down the aisle, pushing and kicking, snarling at the congregation to stay in their seats. Pontius Pilate takes a seat in front of the church.*

NARRATOR: Pilate called together the chief priests, the rulers, and the people, and said to them:

PILATE: You brought me this man as one who was inciting the people to rebellion. I have examined him in your presence and have found no basis for your charges against him. I find no fault with this man. Neither has Herod, for he sent him back to us. As you can see, he has done nothing to deserve death. Therefore I will punish him and then release him (Luke 23:13–17).

Pilate freezes with a whip in his hands and the choir sings "Crucify Him" (from the Easter Song*).*

NARRATOR: Wanting to release Jesus, Pilate appealed to the people again. But they kept shouting "Crucify him! Crucify him!" For the third time he spoke to them, saying:

PILATE: I find no fault with this man. Why? What crime has this man committed? Therefore I will have him punished and then release him.

NARRATOR: But with loud shouts the people insistently demanded that he be crucified, and their shouts prevailed. Pilate granted their demands.

The choir sings "Behold My Savior Now Is Taken" (from the St. Matthew's Passion*)*.

NARRATOR: For it is written, and so it shall be told: He was oppressed and afflicted, yet he did not open his mouth, he was lead away like a lamb to the slaughter, and as a sheep before her shearers is silent, so he did not open his mouth (Isaiah 53:7).

Jesus is led away down the aisle and everyone departs from the front of the stage except the choir and narrator. The actors take seats in the sanctuary for the remainder of the ceremony. Jesus returns to the altar unnoticed and will talk over the storm sound effects.

NARRATOR: So the soldiers took charge of Jesus. Carrying his own cross, he went out to the place of the skull. Here they crucified him, and with him two others—one on each side, with Jesus in the middle. Pilate had a notice prepared and fastened to the cross. It read: Jesus of Nazareth, The King of the Jews. Many of the Jews read the sign, for the place where Jesus was crucified was near the city, and the sign was written in Aramaic, Latin, and Greek. The chief priests of the Jews protested to Pilate, "Do not write 'The King of the Jews.' " Pilate answered, "What I have written, I have written." When the soldiers crucified Jesus, they took his clothes, dividing them into four shares, one for each of them, with the undergarment remaining. "Let's not tear it," they said to one another. "Let's decide by lot who will get it." This happened that the scripture might be fulfilled which said: "They divided my garments among them and cast lots for my clothing." Sit with me. Watch and pray. For the hour comes that the Savior shall give his life so that you may live. Sit with me. Watch and pray.

Everyone sits in silence for at least five minutes. The storm sound effects rage on. After five minutes the choir sings "Lamb of God" (from the St. Matthew's Passion*). After the song, the storm sound effects continue for several more minutes.*

JESUS: Father, forgive them for they know not what they do.

John rises with Mary and stands in front of the middle cross.

JESUS: Dear Mother, behold thy son. John, behold thy mother.

They stand crying and holding one another and then slowly return to their seats. The choir sings "Although" (from the St. Matthew's Passion*)*

JESUS: I thirst!

The sanctuary should be darkened with spotlights focused on the crosses.

NARRATOR: Immediately one of them ran and got a sponge. He filled it with wine vinegar, put it on a stick, and offered it to Jesus to drink. The rest said, "Now leave him alone. Let's see if Elijah comes to save him."

One of the criminals who hung there hurled insults at him: "Aren't you the Christ? Save yourself and us too!" But the other criminal rebuked him, "Don't you fear God," he said, "since you are under the same sentence? We are punished justly, for we are getting what our deeds deserve. But

this man has done no wrong." Then he said, "Jesus, remember me when you come into your kingdom."
JESUS: I tell you the truth; today you shall be with me in paradise.

Sharp thunder sounds and the storm sounds intensify. The sound effects continue for the next five minutes.

NARRATOR: At the sixth hour, darkness came over the whole land until the ninth hour. (*The lights on the cross dim.*) And Jesus cried out in a loud voice:
JESUS (*loudly, mournfully, and in great pain*): *Eloi! Eloi! Lama sabachthani.* My God! My God! Why hast thou forsaken me?

More intense sound effects are heard. From the four corners of the sanctuary, the round "When Jesus Wept" is sung. Once again the sound effects continue for five minutes.

JESUS: God, into thy hands I commit my spirit.

The storm rages for another two minutes and then the curtain behind the crosses is torn in half to the sound of a loud clap of thunder.

JESUS: It is finished!

The storm continues to rage.

NARRATOR: Surely this man was the child of God.

The soloist sings "Cavalry."

NARRATOR: Leave this place. Watch and pray. For truly he was the child of God.

All doors to the sanctuary open as the congregation files out in silence. The solo is sung over and over until everyone has departed.

Easter Sunrise Celebration

Background

This service can occur outside at 5:30 or 6:00 A.M., just before the sun rises. It is a joyous celebration of victory in the faith.

The Ceremony

Pastoral Prayer

Living and Holy God, God of the resurrection, we raise our humble prayers to you this morning, thanking you for the daybreak and the dawn. We thank you for the gifts of this resurrection Sunday. May our hearts, minds, and souls be renewed for service to thee. May the sweet and blessed Spirit of transformation and renewal go with us, be in us, and abide through us now and forever. May the light and love of your Spirit illuminate our paths and provide us with renewed energy, determination, and faith to be your faithful servants in this world you have created. We thank you, for Christ has risen! We love you, for Christ has risen! We rededicate ourselves to you in the spirit of our resurrected Savior, Jesus Christ. Amen.

Scripture Readings
- Luke 24:1–12
- John 20:1–9

Sunrise Litany

MINISTER: As the sun in the heavens rises, we also rise as people of God. As the son of man rises from the grave, we also rise as the people of God.

PEOPLE: Let us give thanks for the spirit of the Resurrection, the spirit of renewal and continuity, the spirit of change and transformation!

MINISTER: The grave no longer is the final resting place of those in Christ. Christ has taken the sting from death and victoriously triumphed over it!

PEOPLE: As followers, we follow Christ beyond the grave. We, too, claim victory over the powers of evil and the sting of death. We, too, rise with Jesus in spirit and power as we live the legacy for future generations.

MINISTER: In the spirit of our ancestors, who rose and triumphed over every calamity and every adversity, every problem and every difficulty, we, too, rise as the people of God in the spirit of our ancestors!

PEOPLE: As a proud people who have borne our share of sorrows and grief, we celebrate that victorious, resilient, triumphant spirit manifested in our ancestors, bequeathed in Christ.

ALL: May we continue to rise in the spirit of Christ and the Easter experience. May we rise over pain and penalty, persecution and prosecution, agony, calamity, and every indemnity which pushes us backward, sequesters our spirits, dashes our hopes, and quenches our joy and determination to live freely, expectantly, proudly, and faithfully! As the suns rises in the heavens, we, too, rise. As Christ our savior and liberator rises, we, too, as the people of God, continue to rise. Rise up, people of God, and claim your strength. Rise up, people of God, and live out your faith! Rise up, people of God, and be true to the spirit of the Resurrection. In Jesus' name, we raise our humble praise and adoration. Amen!

The Proclamation

This truly is the day the Lord has made. Let us rejoice and be glad in it. Easter is a day of transition, rebirth, and born-again faith. It is an opportunity for us to review our past transgressions and look toward the greater glory of our futures—to truly be repentant for our sins and be born again in faith, integrity, and strength.

Music

- ◆ He Arose
- ◆ This Little Light of Mine
- ◆ O How I Love Jesus
- ◆ Glory, Glory Hallelujah

Closing Prayer

MINISTER: Dear God, we thank you that your only child arose for us. As Christ goes with us and lives among us, may we bear witness to the eternal light that Jesus brought to us. May we continue to rise in the spirit of love, truth, forgiveness, reconciliation, and redemption. Grant us the mind, spirit, and will to bear testimony to your eternal life among us so that we may live in grace and peace. Amen.

An Easter Forensic for Youth

Background

Ceremonies that involve youth allow them to become an integral part of their church community. It is important that they understand the traditions of their church in order to improve them and pass them on to their children. The following is a ceremony that was spontaneously put together by the eighth through twelfth grade Sunday school class at Hope United Methodist Church. We call the class the Sunday school class of What's Happenin' Now. Each year the Sunday school classes put together a fifteen-minute presentation for Easter. The 1996 class was encouraged to do something different and came up with a forensic presentation. They coordinated the movements and the staging. This presentation created a powerful message. For this particular forensic, students created their own lines. The theme was the upper room.

Participants

♦ As many or as few students can participate as are available.

The Ceremony

The disciples have gathered to discuss whether or not Christ is risen. As the ceremony begins, the youth are scattered about the stage.

STUDENT 1: So what's the deal about Jesus?

STUDENT 2: He's dead!

STUDENT 3: We'll be dead too!

STUDENT 4: You know his body has disappeared?

STUDENT 5: But a dead body can't walk!

STUDENT 6: Yes it can, when it's Jesus!

STUDENT 7: Well I'm not going to believe it until he comes in my face and I can put my fingers through the hole in his side.

STUDENT 8: He said he would return.

STUDENT 9: He made believers out of us all. He taught us everything is possible. He wouldn't've brought us this far to leave us here.

STUDENT 10: I'm with Thomas! He's not coming back!

STUDENT 11: I believe Christ will come again!

STUDENT 12: Christ is dead! I saw him fall. They buried him. And that's final.

Chaos breaks out. Everyone is talking and moving at once. Finally the players form a V with one student at the center. The believers are on one side and the doubters on the other.

BELIEVERS (*in unison*): He's alive!

DOUBTERS (*in unison*): We saw him die!

BELIEVERS (*in unison*): He's alive!

DOUBTERS (*in unison*): We saw him die!

BELIEVERS (*in unison*): He's alive!

DOUBTERS (*in unison*): We saw him die!

BELIEVERS (*in unison*): Christ is risen!

DOUBTERS (*in unison*): We saw him fall!

BELIEVERS (*in unison*): Christ is risen!

DOUBTERS (*in unison*): We saw him fall!

BELIEVERS (*in unison*): Christ is risen!

DOUBTERS (*in unison*): We saw him fall!

STUDENT 2: Stop! Everybody!

STUDENT 1: Look, why are you all being so irrational? He said he'd be back, so what's the problem?

STUDENT 2: Irrational! Ya'll talking about a dead guy with holes in his side comin' back and taking us to some glory land! Who's being irrational?!

STUDENT 5: Look, I'm scared! You know the soldiers are going to come and catch us if we stay here!

STUDENT 6: Not with Jesus by our side.

STUDENT 10: What! A dead man? I don't think so!

STUDENT 9: Christ is more than just a man. He is the spirit of everlasting life.

STUDENT 10: Look, I'm not leaving my family and home for no dead man!

STUDENT 1: How you gonna say something like that, especially after being with him for three years and all that he's taught us! Look we saw him get put in his tomb.

STUDENT 9: But we walk by faith and not by sight.

STUDENT 3: Dead or alive, we gottsa go!

Chaos breaks out again, with the disciples arguing among themselves. Suddenly one calls out in surprise.

STUDENT 9: My Lord, it's you!

The student in the center of the V looks offstage. The rest of the group turns to look at the student. Then Student 5 gasps and points in the direction that the center student is looking. Slowly the group follows his or her hand. Surprised expressions cross their faces, and they all sink to the floor on their knees, still staring.

ALL: Christ is risen!

Mother's Day Celebration

Background

The best way we have found to describe Mother's Day was a greeting card that thanked Mom for what she did *not* do. This celebration capitalizes on that theme, while clearly defining mothers as heroes. This idea rings true when you think about mothers who go without food to make sure their children have enough, who wear old clothes or tattered underwear while their children are presentable and shining, who forego sleep so they can be at their child's bedside in the wink of an eye if he or she stirs or cries, and mothers who do not walk away when a child's wrong but makes the child pay for his or her indiscretions behind closed doors. As adults we can look back over our lives and remember all the things our mothers did and did not do.

Mother's Day is one of those times when people begin to express feelings and emotions about parenting and sacrifices. It is important for children of all ages to express these ideas, but particularly important for teenagers.

Provide a lot of encouragement for the youth. An ideal group for the ceremony is the eighth through twelfth grade Sunday school class because it is already an intact group. It is a smaller sample of all the teens in the church. Their participation may also serve to recruit more youth to your Sunday school.

A Note about Teens

Adolescence marks a time in the lives of teens when they want to pull away from parents and are beginning to strike out on their own to find their independence. They try to show themselves as individuals who can make decisions and exercise their rights. Overall, this is often a very tumultuous period. This celebration gives teenagers an opportunity to let Mom know that they still care despite their attitudes and behaviors. Our theme is mothers as heroes. The best way to introduce this idea to teenagers is to tell them they will go before the church and simply say in their own words, "Mom, you're my hero because . . ." Anticipate the resistance—"I don't want to do it; you can't make me do it"—but stand firm. If necessary, say, "Well, you don't have to, but you will be the only kid whose mom will be sitting in the congregation knowing that you are in the Sunday school class and you chose not to do it. We won't say you have to do it. It's just important that you think about it. All you would do is just state very briefly why your mom is your hero." We encourage teens to think about this the week before and invite their mothers to be in the audience.

We recommended that this ceremony be a part of the church service. It can also be held at a banquet, luncheon, or breakfast where moms are present and the children come forward on a stage.

Usually this ceremony is very emotional and very provocative for both children and parents because all—especially teens—are struggling. They have had their ups and downs. To hear their child finally say in essence, "Mom, I love you and you are my hero because . . ." sends a powerful message, especially on Mother's Day.

Bring tissues.

Participants

+ Sunday school teacher or coordinator
+ mothers
+ children

Materials

+ a plant, flower, or gift for every mother
+ tissues

In Advance

+ Announce the ceremony at least a week ahead of time, so children can plan what they will say.
+ Discuss, if necessary, the kinds of things children might want to say to their mothers.
+ Issue special invitations to the mothers.
+ Gather plants, flowers, or small gifts for children to give their mothers. Have some extra gifts on hand.

The Ceremony

The Introduction

The children are called from the audience to stand in a line on the stage. The Sunday school teacher or coordinator defines for the congregation his or her thoughts about heroes and the importance of letting mothers know why they are heroes.

The Words

Each youth in turn comes to the microphone and says "Mom, you are my hero because . . ." and then returns to his or her place in line.

After the last child has spoken, play a very moving and powerful song such as "Wind Beneath My Wings" by Bette Midler or Gladys Knight.

The Presentation

As the music plays, the Sunday school teacher or coordinator speaks.

TEACHER OR COORDINATOR: Will the mother of (*youth's name*) please stand up.

The mother stands and the child takes a plant, flower, or gift, walks to where she is, and gives her the gift along with a hug. By this time, parents and youth are usually crying and feeling very emotional. The youth remains with his or her mother. The ceremony continues until every mother is standing and has received a gift and a hug from her child.

The Closing

TEACHER OR COORDINATOR: Happy Mother's Day!

Father's Day Celebration

Background

A long time ago, when things were different, it was thought that a father's role was to be an unemotional breadwinner. Fathers had little to do with raising the children, and the fathers were always too busy for the children anyway. Designing the Father's Day Celebration proved to be a complex task. Repeating the Mother's Day Celebration did not work. A number of the teens were even more adamant about refusing to express sentiment to their fathers. Then, at a youth summit, we asked teens to discuss how they would like their parents to become more involved in their education. Instead, the discussion turned to ways their parents could become more involved with them personally. From a number of young men we heard that they wanted their fathers to tell them they cared. That discussion became the basis of the Father's Day Celebration.

Father's Day is another occasion when we don't always take the opportunity to express feelings and emotions in an open setting. As in the Mother's Day ritual, we decided to encourage people to let one another know how they feel. But this time the celebration was reversed. For Father's Day, we asked the fathers to tell their children how they feel about them.

Preferably the celebration will be held at the church during the Father's Day service, but a banquet or fellowship hall during a breakfast, lunch, or dinner would do as well. The target group is fathers of teenagers.

Participants

- children
- their fathers
- coordinator

Materials

- boutonniere for each father

In Advance

- Talk with each father prior to the ceremony, both to make sure the father plans to attend and to give him an opportunity to think about what to say.
- Tell the fathers that they will be asked to finish the sentence "If I could . . ." and encourage them to plan their words ahead of time.

The Ceremony

As the ceremony begins, the youth will stand at the back of the church or hall, each carrying a boutonniere to pin on his or her father's lapel.

Calling the Fathers

All the fathers are called to the stage or altar. The coordinator talks briefly about the role of fathers in their children's lives.

COORDINATOR (*to each father in turn*): Please look at your child and complete the sentence "If I could . . ."

Be prepared for some fathers to become very emotional because they often do not have an opportunity to express feelings to their children. After all fathers have completed the sentence, play the song "If I Could" as the coordinator speaks.

COORDINATOR (*to each child in turn*): Will the (*daughter/son*) of (*name*) please pin your boutonniere on your father's lapel.

As they are called, the youth walk down the aisle and pin the boutonnieres on their fathers' shirts. It is not necessary to wait until each youth has finished before calling the next person. The youth should pin on the flowers and then give their fathers a hug. During this celebration we have been impressed with how emotional both father and youth become. We have seen tears and heard statements of forgiveness and declarations of "I'll be there for you." This is really important to both the fathers and the youth because it represents an opportunity for fathers to express to their children all those feelings that they do not often take the opportunity to say.

The Closing

COORDINATOR: Happy Father's Day!

A Litany of Thanksgiving

Background

While Americans annually celebrate Thanksgiving on the fourth Thursday of the year, African traditional society views thanksgiving as a perpetual acknowledgment of the enduring goodness of God. Giving thanks to God for our many blessings is not something celebrated at a particular time each year. In predominantly agrarian communities, where farming is the prominent vocation and people live directly off the land, thus relying more on the natural elements for prosperity, we find more rituals, rites, and ceremonies of praise and thanksgiving. While the element of thanksgiving is included in many religious rituals and rites in African belief systems and prayers, this ritual-litany can be recited in worship or in a separate thanksgiving observance in the home or church.

Participants

- ◆ leader
- ◆ congregation

In Advance

- ◆ Prepare and distribute copies of the litany.

The Ceremony

Note that in this ritual the content of litany is reversed for leader and people.

LEADER: To thee, O God, we give thanks!

PEOPLE: For the good earth, the sun, the moon, and stars, and rain.

LEADER: To thee, O God, we give thanks!

PEOPLE: For planting and harvesting, for sowing and reaping, for seed and soil, plants and livestock.

LEADER: To thee, O God, we give thanks!

PEOPLE: For the breath of life and the breath of air, for the presence of life in wind, seas, rocks, and air.

LEADER: To thee, O God, we give thanks!

PEOPLE: For the gift of life and the gift of love, for the love of life and a life of love.

LEADER: To thee, O God, we give thanks!

PEOPLE: For the gifts of mind, body, soul, and spirit, the gifts of individuals, communities, villages, and nations.

LEADER: To thee, O God, we give thanks!

PEOPLE: For the gifts of ingenuity and industry, innovation, creativity, and dexterity.

LEADER: To thee, O God, we give thanks!

PEOPLE: For the gifts of unity, culture, spirituality, and diversity.

LEADER: To thee, O God, we give thanks!

PEOPLE: For the gifts of families, children, extended families, and others.

LEADER: To thee, O God, we give thanks!

PEOPLE: For the gifts of music, song, dance, and praise, the gifts of genius, intelligence, and common sense these days.

LEADER: To thee, O God, we give thanks!

PEOPLE: For the strength and perseverance of our people and ancestors who braved storms and winds, fires and whirlwinds.

LEADER: To thee, O God, we give thanks!

PEOPLE: For the promises of living and the living of these days, for the Christ who lives in us and we who live in Christ!

LEADER: To thee, O God, we give thanks!

PEOPLE: For the gifts of the church, of prophecies and tongues, for the gifts of illumination, teaching, and the spirit of one.

LEADER: To thee, O God, we give thanks!

ALL: As the people of God of African descent, let us praise God forever for our means of ascent; for spirit, for love, for strength and power, we praise thee, O God, for the gifts of the hour. All praises and thanks be to the God of life, who loves, sustains, energizes, and transforms us now and always. Amen.

Christmas Celebration:
The Gifts of the Magi

Background

I n the Christian faith, Christ is God's ultimate gift to us and our celebration of Jesus' birth symbolizes our willingness to share our Christ gifts with others. We believe that the place and peoples of Africa have had a significant role in the formation and gifting of the Christian belief. For example, we know that the religion of the ancient Hebrews is one cornerstone in the foundation of Christian faith. The Ten Commandments, which may be derived from the negative confessions of Egypt, have carried over into Christian belief. The Hebrews spent hundreds of years in Egypt, and numerous historians believe that the Hebrews were comprised largely of black Africans. Joseph, when warned in a dream that Herod was seeking to kill Jesus, fled to Egypt for safety. The Jewish historian Josephus describes Jesus as *melanchrous,* which means "having dark or black skin."[1] Egypt and Ethiopia are mentioned countless times in the Bible. Thus the African influence is invariably present.

A biblical narrative reminiscent of African influences is the story of the three Magi who come to Jesus bearing gifts. While it is presumed that the Magi traveled from Persia or some distant place in the East, they brought gold, frankincense, and myrrh, which were precious commodities in many nations that traded in Africa, since the lands and nations were mineral rich.

More significant, however, is the African tradition of the elders or wise ones seeking knowledge and wisdom from children. Often African elders traveled long distances to greet a child at birth to obtain new insight for the future. African proverbs purport that true knowledge and wisdom can be found in children, who happen to be our greatest teachers. Even greater knowledge is received from the chosen or anointed ones. Thus the presentation of gifts by the Magi to Jesus is equally for the attainment of more wisdom, which is in keeping with the best of African tradition. The Magi's gifts not only show adoration and praise for the Christchild, but are also emblems of a deeper knowledge and wisdom, mystically exchanged in their Christ encounter. The Magi's stubborn refusal to return to Herod to disclose the whereabouts of Jesus may be the fruits of a deeper knowledge and insight acquired from their visit with the Christchild.

Moreover, the Magi's mysterious presence, their long sojourning to Christ, and sudden quixotic disappearance evidence remnants of African folk traditions which speak of mythical strangers appearing in villages bearing gifts for the chosen and then vanishing.[2] The almost magical and numinous nature of their presence at the birth of Christ, along with the fact that they followed a star to the birthplace, underscores the cosmic significance of Christ's birth, which also hints of African influences.

This ritual of the birth of Jesus dramatizes the deeds and gifts of the three Magi and the significance of retrieving and preserving the African elements in telling the story of Jesus' birth from this viewpoint in the African American church.

Participants

+ the three Magi (2 males and 1 female)
+ narrator

Materials

+ a makeshift cradle in a manger with a "child" wrapped in swaddling cloths, if available
+ African attire
+ music
+ offering basket

The Ceremony

All the people of the village gather for the celebration wearing African attire. Music may be played for the occasion as the people prepare for the dramatization. The ceremony may occur on a stage or in a fellowship hall or an auditorium. The scene is a makeshift cradle in a manger with a "child" wrapped in swaddling cloths. If props are not available, the cradle and manger can be imaginary.

NARRATOR: We have come to tell the story of Jesus' birth. We have come to celebrate the successful journey of the

Magi to the Christchild. We have come bearing precious gifts. Each gift marks some important characteristic of African peoples. Each gift embodies an ancient truth and wisdom which the Magi believe has been exemplified by Africans and will be further personified in the life of the Christchild as the savior of the people.

The Magi now enter the room, each bearing a different gift for presentation to the child. Each of the Magi bows in humble adoration in presenting the gift. In departure from biblical tradition, but in recapturing the inclusiveness of African tradition, the Magi are portrayed by two men and one woman.

FIRST OF THE MAGI: We have come to you, O Wise and Precious One, after many days and nights of hard journeying. We have come braving the storm clouds of opposition and adversity. We have come knowing that you have brought and sustained us through this journey. We have come knowing you are the source of hope, wisdom, strength, and joy of our people. We have come to present you with the gifts of our people.

The first gift is gold. Gold is one of the most precious resources of the earth. It is found in abundance on the mother continent. Gold symbolizes the many gifts of our people. It is soft; which means it can be shaped into many forms without losing its value. Gold signifies our enduring value as a people. We have been tried by fire. We have been shaped and molded by many forces in the universe and have not lost our value and strength as a people. Gold can be changed into many forms. Gold can be smelted. Whatever form it takes, gold never loses value. It retains its durability,

pliability, and usefulness. And so it is with our people. Over
the centuries we have been shaped into many forms, but we
retain our value in the eyes of God, in the eyes of the earth,
and in the eyes of the heavens. We know also, Wise One,
that we shall never lose value in your eyes, for the promise
of your reign is like gold to us.

Gold also has "light"—it does not lose its luster.
Whatever is mixed with it, the gold always comes shining
through. And so it is with our people. We retain our luster,
our light, our shining radiance in the mix of many realities.
Our true nature; our strength, our soul, our spirit, our desire to walk and be in the light always irradiates the presence of things obscured in the shadows.

You, O Wise One, shall never lose your shining radiance and brilliance, for you are the light of our people. You,
O Wise One, embody all the truth and love that true light
brings in a world of shadows.

We traveled much of our journey by night, following
the light, the star from the East which rested over this
place. We have come bringing the light, but also seeking
the light that you embody. Like gold, may you and our
people forever keep the brilliance of light and the perma-
nency of unending value in all things and at all times. We
honor you with this gift of precious Nubian gold. Please receive it, O Wise One, in the spirit of our people and in the
spirit of things to come in your reign. We offer this gold as
a symbol of what you mean to us and of what we shall be
and attain through you.

*The first of the three Magi kisses the child and stands. Music
may be played as the congregation stands and sings "Go Tell It*

*on the Mountain," "Joy to the World," or some other seasonal
music. The second of the three Magi steps forward to the cradle,
bows, and offers the gift of frankincense.)*

SECOND OF THE MAGI (*a woman*): Spiritual One, we come
bringing frankincense in praise and adoration of you.
Incense symbolizes the sweet fragrance of your holy presence and the sweet redolence of the legacy of our people.
The vaporous smoke of the incense signifies the spirit of
our people, effervescent and unbounded by material or
fleshly limitations.

The sweet fragrance of your blessed spirit and the spirit
of our people can never be wholly contained or subject to
the things of this earth, for they are eternal, without permanent form but imbuing permanent essence to the hearts,
minds, and souls of God's people.

Those malodorous realities which often waft their way
into our memories and senses as a people of God, realities
which bind, shame, and destroy our people, are dispelled by
the frankincense of your presence. For too long we have
been surrounded by the foul smells of hatred, disunity, envy,
jealousy, discord, persecution, prosecution, alienation, and
extermination. These realities forever divide and polarize the
people of God. This frankincense symbolizes the power of
your presence in dissipating the things which keep us from
being all you would have us to be. O Spiritual One, please
accept this humble offering and oblation to you. We offer
this gift of frankincense as a symbol of what you mean to us
and what we shall be and attain through you.

*The second of the three Magi kisses the child and rises. Here
more music may be played as the congregation stands and*

sings "We Three Kings," "O Come All Ye Faithful," or other music of your choice. The third of the three Magi walks toward the cradle, kneels, and offers a pouch of myrrh.

THIRD OF THE MAGI: Anointed One of Healing, we have come to present the gift of myrrh. Mixed with other substances, it is used for healing and anointing. May the wounds, pains, suffering, and calamities of our people be redeemed through your presence. May you realize all the healing and anointing powers the great God gives you. May you continue to pour out your spirit of health and wholeness upon us as we seek to be like you in all things.

Myrrh is an essential element of many medicines. May you as the master healer and physician be an essential part of the hope, faith, and health of our people. May you heal, anoint, and restore them to their rightful and wholesome place despite their many wounds.

O Anointed One, we raise our humble adoration to you because in you resides all hope. Through you we realize the power, presence, and gifts of healing, and by you we receive our promise for the future. We offer this gift of myrrh as a symbol of what you mean to us and what we shall be and attain through you.

The third of the three Magi kisses the child and stands. The congregation rises and sings "Away in a Manger," "Silent Night," "Angels We Have Heard on High," or other music. Then the Magi all bow and leave the stage or room.

NARRATOR: As the Magi have offered the precious gifts of their people to the Christchild as a symbol of what he means to them and what they hope to receive through him,

let the people of God come forth to offer their precious
gifts to the baby Jesus. These gifts will be used to further
the mission and ministry of Christ's church, to reach others
in need, and to help us all realize the gifts that Christ has
called us to use and to realize as we serve in Christ's name.

The congregation comes forward and offers gifts to the
Christchild.

The Closing
The ceremony may be closed with prayer or music such as
"Go Tell It on the Mountain," "We Three Kings," or other
familiar tunes.

Glossary

Akan In the fourteenth century when Europeans, especially the Portuguese, arrived on the coast of what is now Ghana, they called all Africans there Akan. Many different though related cultural groups came under the Akan umbrella.

Asante, Molef Professor, Department of African American Studies, Temple University. Pioneer in the Afrocentric movement

Asantewa, Yaa The Queen Mother of the Ashanti who led a rebellion against the British in 1900

Asente (Ashanti) Tribe on the Gold Coast of Africa

as salaam alaikum Peace be unto you

buba Traditional dress of some African males

Denkera One of the original states in the sixteenth century that composed the Ashanti Kingdom

Dogon A people of the Sudan whose cosmogony, metaphysics, and religion have been equated with the peoples of antiquity

Durkheim, Emile (1815–1917) French sociologist and philosopher

Fordham, Monroe Former assistant professor of history at State University College, Buffalo

Habari Gani Ki-swahili word which means "What is the news?"

Ibo Tribe located in Nigeria

imani Faith

Karenga, Maulana Creator and father of the African American celebration of Kwanzaa

kiini Core

kikombe cha umoja The unity cup used during Kwanzaa

kinara Candleholder for the seven candles used during Kwanzaa

kujichagulia Self-determination

Kumasi Original African state ruled by Osei Tutu in the late 1600s which later became part of the Ashanti Kingdom

kusifu litany of tribute

kuumba Creativity

Kwanzaa An African American holiday developed by Dr. Maulana Karenga to celebrate the first fruits

mahali patakatifu-au pa salama Central location of the house

Mann, Kenny She grew up in Nairobi, Kenya, studying zoology there then filmmaking in England. She has written documentary films and worked as a freelance journalist.

matangazo Telling the story

mazao Fruits and vegetables, which symbolize the rewards of collective labor

Mbiti, John S. Expert in African religions and philosophy. Formally professor of religious studies at Makerere University, Uganda, and director of the Ecumenical Institute, Bossey, Switzerland.

mkeka Straw placemat used during Kwanzaa which symbolizes the tradition and history of the African American. All other symbols are placed on the mkeka.

mkutano The Gathering

moyo Heart

mshumaa saba The seven candles that symbolizes the principles of Kwanzaa

muhindi An ear of corn used during the Kwanzaa celebration to represent each child

Nguzo Saba Seven principles of blackness

nia Purpose

n'sah To drink

nyumba House blessing

Richards, Dona Associate professor, Department of Black and Puerto Rican Studies, Hunter College, City University of New York

sadaka The offering of gifts

Sankofa An Akan philosophy that means "in order to know where you are going you must know where you have been"

sasa A phase of life according to African religion that covers the "now period"

Turner, Victor Symbolic anthropologist

Tutu, Osei Founder of the Ashanti Kingdom who received the golden stool from heaven in about 1670

ujamaa Cooperative economics

ujima Collective works and responsibility

ukarimu Hospitality

ukitazama utaviona If you look you will see them

umoja Unity

wa alaikum salaam And peace be unto you

wamesimama They are rising up

watu wote na wajue Let all the people know

zamani A phase of life according to African religion which is a period beyond which nothing can go. The termination of life.

zawadi Gifts that are given on the seventh day of Kwanzaa

Notes

Introduction

1. Molefi Asante, *Malcolm X as Cultural Hero and Other Afrocentric Essays* (Trenton, N.J.: Africa World Press, 1993), 37–44.

2. Carlyle Fielding Stewart III, *Soul Survivors: An African American Spirituality* (Louisville: Westminster John Knox, 1997).

The Significance of African-based Rituals in the African American Church

1. Dona Richards, "The Implications of African American Spirituality," in *African Culture: The Rhythms of Unity,* ed. Molefi Asante and Kariamu Welsh Asante (Trenton, N.J.: Africa World Press, 1990), 217. See also Molefi Asante, *The Afrocentric Idea* (Philadelphia: Temple University Press, 1987).

2. Victor Turner, *The Ritual Process* (New York: Cornell University, 1969), 94–95.

3. Monroe Fordham, *Major Themes in Northern Black Religious Thought, 1800–1860* (New York: Exposition Press, 1975), 3.

4. Richards, "The Implications of African American Spirituality," 217.

5. Emile Durkheim, *The Division of Labor in Society* (New York: Macmillan, 1933). See the discussion of mechanical and organic solidarity (pp. 70–132).

The Common Elements of African American Ceremonies and Celebrations

1. The word *Sankofa* comes from Akan. When Europeans arrived on the coast of what is Ghana today, they called all the Africans located there Akan (AH´ kahn), even though these people were comprised of

many different—though related—cultural groups. Kenny Mann, *The Guinea Coast: Oyo, Benin, Ashanti,* African Kingdoms of the Past Series (Parsippany, N.J.: Dillon Press, 1996), 7, 77.

2. John S. Mbiti, *African Religions and Philosophies* (Portsmouth, N.H.: Heinemann Educational Publishers, 1969).

Baptism

1. John S. Mbiti, *Introduction to African Religion* (Oxford: Heinemann International, 1989), 148.

2. Marcel Griaule, *Conversations with Ogotemmeli: An Introduction to Dogon Religious Ideas* (London: Oxford, 1980), 19.

Rites of Passage

1. Kelvin L. Seifert and Robert S. Hoffnung, *Child and Adolescent Development* (Boston: Houghton Mifflin Co., 1987), 591.

The Wedding Ceremony

1. Andy Langsford, *Christian Weddings: Resources to Make Your Wedding Unique* (Nashville: Abingdon, 1995), 30.

2. Ibid., 35.

3. Ibid., 59.

4. Ibid., 65–68.

Funeral Ceremony: A Celebration of Life

1. Mbiti, *African Religions and Philosophies,* 24.

Kwanzaa Celebration

1. James C. Anyike, *African American Holidays* (Chicago: Popular Truth, 1991), 72.

The Tools of Freedom Ceremony

1. Frederick Douglass, *Narrative of the Life of an American Slave* (New York: Penguin Books USA, 1968), 49.

2. Frederick Douglass, *My Bondage and My Freedom* (New York: Dover Publications, 1969), 406.

3. William Loren Katz, *Black People Who Made the Old West* (Trenton, N.J.: Africa World Press, 1992).

4. Columbus Salley, *The Black One Hundred: A Ranking of the Most Influential African Americans, Past and Present* (New York: Citadel Press Book, 1993–94).

Christmas Celebration: The Gifts of the Magi

1. Robert Eisler, *The Messiah Jesus and John the Baptist* (London: Methuen and Co., 1931).

2. Paul Radin, ed., *African Folktales*, Bollingen Series (Princeton: Princeton University Press, 1952); Harold Courlander, *A Treasury of Afro-American Folklore* (New York: Crown, 1976); Henry D. Spalding, ed., *Encyclopedia of Black Folklore and Humor* (New York: Jonathan David Publishers, 1990); Carlyle Fielding Stewart III, *Conversations with African Friends: Recollections of African Folk Wisdom (1970–1990),* unpublished manuscript.

References

Adams, Russell L. *Great Negroes Past and Present.* 3d. ed. Chicago: Afro-Am Publishing Co., 1984.

African Heritage Study Bible. Nashville: John Winston Publisher, 1993.

Anyike, James C. *African American Holidays.* Chicago: Popular Truth, 1991.

Arnoitt, Kathleen. *African Myths and Legends.* Oxford: Oxford University Press, 1994.

Asante, Molefi. *Malcolm X as Cultural Hero and Other Afrocentric Essays.* Trenton, N.J.: Africa World Press, 1993.

Asante, Molefi, and Kariamu Asante. *African Culture: The Rhythms of Unity.* Trenton, N.J.: Africa World Press, 1990.

Beattie, John. *Bunyoro: An African Kingdom.* New York: Holt Rinehart and Winston, 1960.

Davidson, Basil. *The African Slave Trade.* Boston: Little, Brown and Co., 1980.

Dixon, Christa K. *Negro Spirituals.* Philadelphia: Fortress Press, 1976.

Douglass, Frederick. *My Bondage and My Freedom.* New York: Dover Publications, 1969.

———. *Narrative of the Life of an American Slave.* New York: Penguin Books USA, 1968.

Felder, Cain Hope. *Troubling Biblical Waters.* Maryknoll, N.Y.: Orbis Books, 1989.

Fordham, Monroe. *Major Themes in Northern Black Religious Thought, 1800–1860.* Hicksville, N.Y.: Exposition Press, 1975.

Gospel Pearls. Nashville: Sunday School Publishing Board, National Baptist Convention, 1921.

Griaule, Marcel. *Conversations with Ogotemmeli: An Introduction to Dogon Religious Ideas.* Oxford: Oxford University Press, 1980.

Haley, Alex. *Roots.* New York: Doubleday and Company, 1976.

Hitchens, Melvin, Sr. *The Black Family and Marriage: A Black Man's Perspective.* New York: Welstar Publications, 1992.

Idowu, E. Bolaji. *African Traditional Religion.* New York: Orbis Books, 1975.

Jackson, Kennell. *America Is Me.* New York: HarperCollins, 1996.

Katz, William L. *Black People Who Made the Old West.* Trenton, N.J.: Africa World Press, 1992.

Langsford, Andy. *Christian Weddings: Resouces to Make Your Wedding Unique.* Nashville: Abingdon, 1995.

Lawson, E. Thomas. *Religions of Africa.* New York: Harper and Row, 1985.

Leslau, Charlotte, and Wolf Leslau. *African Proverbs.* White Plains, N.Y.: Peter Pauper Press Book, 1985.

Life Application Bible. Wheaton, Ill., and Grand Rapids, Mich.: Tyndale House Publishers and Zondervan Publishing House, 1991.

Mann, Kenny. *The Guinea Coast: Oyo, Benin, Ashanti.* African Kingdoms of the Past Series. Parsippany, N.J.: Dillon Press, 1996.

Mbiti, John S. *African Religions and Philosophies.* Portsmouth, N.H.: Heinemann Educational Publishers, 1969.

———. *Introduction to African Religion.* Oxford, England: Heinemann International, 1989.

———. *The Prayers of African Religion.* New York: Orbis Books, 1975.

Mullane, Deirdre, ed. *Crossing the Danger Water: Three Hundred Years of African-American Writing.* New York: Doubleday, 1993.

Neel, Steven M. "Say I Do." In *The Wedding Ceremony.* Colorado Springs: Meriwether Publishing, 1995.

New Revised Standard Version of the Bible. Nashville: Thomas Nelson, 1989.

Pakenham, Thomas. *The Scramble for Africa: White Man's Conquest of the Dark Continent from 1876 to 1912.* New York: Avon Books, 1991.

Perrott, D. V. *Concise Swahili and English Dictionary.* New York: David McKay, 1972.

Petry, Ann. *Harriet Tubman: Conductor on the Underground Railroad.* New York: HarperCollins, 1983.

Richards, Dona. "The Implications of African American Spirituality." In *African Culture: The Rhythms of Unity*. Trenton, N.J.: Africa World Press, 1990.

Salley, Columbus. *The Black One Hundred: A Ranking of the Most Influential African Americans, Past and Present*. New York: Citadel Press Book, 1993–94.

Seifert, Kelvin L., and Robert S. Hoffnung. *Child and Adolescent Development*. Boston: Houghton Mifflin Co., 1987.

Shorter, Aylward. *African Christian Spirituality*. New York: Orbis Books, 1978.

————. *Prayer in the Religious Traditions of Africa*. New York: Oxford University Press, 1975.

Somé, Malidoma Patrice. *Ritual, Power, Healing and Community*. Portland, Ore.: Swan and Raven, 1993.

The Songs of Zion. Nashville: Abingdon, 1981.

Stewart, Carlyle Fielding, III. *African American Church Growth*. Nashville: Abingdon, 1994.

————. *Soul Survivors: An African American Spirituality*. Louisville: Westminster John Knox, 1997.

————. *Street Corner Theology*. Nashville: John Winston Publishers, 1996.

Taylor, John. *The Primal Vision*. London: SCM Press, 1963.

Turner, Victor. *The Ritual Process*. Ithaca, N.Y.: Cornell University Press, 1969.

The United Methodist Hymnal. Edited by Carlton R. Young. Nashville: The United Methodist Publishing House, 1989.

Work, John W. *Folk Songs of the American Negro*. Nashville: John W. Work, 1907.

Discography

Blues

Hannibal. *African Portraits*. Teldec, Warner Music, 1995.
John Lee Hooker. *Boom Boom*. Virgin Records, 1992.

Gospel Music

Yolanda Adams. *Through the Storm*. Diadem Records, 1991.
————. *More Than a Melody*. Stud Rico Music, 1994.
Edwin Hawkins. *Music Arts Seminar, Chicago Mass Choir*. Polygram
    Records, 1990.
————. *Face to Face*. Polygram Records, 1990.
The Winans. *Let My People Go*. Qwest Records, 1985.

Jazz

John Coltrane. *Africa Brass*. 2 vols. MCA Records, 1974.
————. *The Best of John Coltrane, His Greatest Years*. MCA Records,
    1982.
————. *Live at the Village Vanguard*. MCA Records, 1987.
————. *A Love Supreme*. MCA Records, 1986.
————. *My Favorite Things*. Atlantic Records, 1961.
————. *Out of This World*. MCA Records, 1987.
Miles Davis. *Kind of Blue*. Columbia/CBS, 1959.
Herbie Hancock. *Speak Like a Child*. Blue Note Records, 1968.
————. *A Tribute to Miles*. Q West Records, 1994.
Wynton Marsalis. *Thick in the South. Soul Gestures in Southern Blue,*
    vol. 1. Sony Music, 1991.
————. *Uptown Ruler. Soul Gestures in Southern Blue,* vol. 2. Sony
    Music, 1991.

————. *Levee Low Moan. Soul Gestures in Southern Blue,* vol. 3. Sony
    Music, 1991.
Randy Scott. *Randy Scott.* R&R Productions, 1994.

Reggae/African Music

African Tribal Music and Dances. Tradition Records, n.d.
The Indestructible Beat of Soweto. Sanaachie Records, 1985.
Bobatunde Olatunji. *Healing Rhythms, Songs and Chants.* Drums of
    Passion Production, n.d.
Bob Marley and The Wailers. *Confrontation.* Island Records. 1983.
————. *Exodus.* Island Records, 1977.
————. *Rastaman Vibrations.* Island Records, 1976.
————. *Uprising.* Island Records, 1980.
Bobby McFerrin. *Medicine Music.* Columbia House, 1990.
Rhythm of Resistance: Music of Black South Africa. Virgin Records,
    1988.